Flower Love

For Aaron:
I'm obsessed with you.

_____

For Hugo and Eoghan:
My eternal loves.

_____

For the Griffiths:
You are
BLACK EXCELLENCE.

_____

For my tribe:
A, D, J, J, J, J, J, R & T:
There were never such devoted sisters.

KRISTEN GRIFFITH-VANDERYACHT

FLOWER LOVE

LUSH FLORAL ARRANGEMENTS FOR THE HEART AND HOME

CLARKSON POTTER/PUBLISHERS
NEW YORK

Contents

WARNING

Working with flowers may cause feelings of happiness, calm, and an increased level of self-worth. Beware, as some flowers may negatively affect your ability to scowl, frown, or anguish. If unwanted feelings of joy persist, immediately put down the flowers and seek out politics.

Introduction

One of the first books I purchased myself was *Making Faces* by Kevyn Aucoin. I will never forget the jaw-dropping transformations he was able to achieve with puffs of pressed powder and flourishes of mascara. *Making Faces* was the perfect slice of escapism as I endured the tragedies of teenager-dom in the nineties. The text was full of trade secrets. It felt like I'd stumbled upon a grimoire of ancient powers, accessing centuries of wisdom without having to do any of the work. It would not be until many years later, when I began instructing floral design, that I would understand there is as much joy and beautiful escape in creating as there is in sharing. Through teaching the art of floral design, I have been able to show my students how to use flowers as a source of healing and beauty. Flowers have changed my life for the better. I know they will change yours as well.

This design resource is for anyone looking to create artful floral arrangements and have fun while they are doing it. The design world can sometimes feel like a cold, judgmental place, which can deter curious creators. Though the floral design recipes offer real instruction, we will never take ourselves too seriously. It's just flowers.

You will also come to learn one of the biggest floral design secrets I have been holding on to for years. (I won't confirm for exactly how long because then you would have enough information to guess my real age, and the last time I checked, the internet thinks I am twenty-nine . . . and I plan to keep it that way!) For now, I want you to adopt the mindset that you belong here just as much as anybody else. In addition to supporting biodiversity and keeping the air on our planet fresh, flowers are here to arouse joy. So, whether you are a professional floral designer, a fledgling creative, or simply love pretty pictures, use this book to enrich your creative life. If you happen to have a laugh (or six) along the way, even better.

The text is divided into three sections: **A Floral Foundation**, **A Rainbow of Arrangements**, and **The Flower Vault**.

In **A Floral Foundation**, you will find all the information needed to get started, including my tips and tricks for crafting color stories, the different parts of an arrangement, my ten floral commandments, and why working with flowers is a form of self-care.

A Rainbow of Arrangements is a color-driven design guide. In this section of the book, arrangements are organized by color and shade. Not the shade you experience when someone is talking about you behind your back, but the kind of shade you can enjoy, like melon, mint, or mauve. Wait, not mauve (for more on that shady lady, see page 245). Each color category includes easy-to-follow instructions for a variety of arrangements and bouquets. These step-by-step floral design recipes demystify all that goes into making an artful arrangement. I mean it when I say *anyone*, even your ditzy roommate who somehow manages to burn boxed mac-n-cheese can use this text to make something pretty.

Each recipe contains three key elements:
1. How to build an organic SHAPE
2. How to layer in COLOR
3. How to create DEPTH

These three elements are the map to creating a multidimensional floral masterpiece. Once acquainted with the techniques, feel free to experiment with *new* shapes, color combinations, and textures of your own design. Coloring outside the lines is highly encouraged. The sooner you learn to listen to and trust your creative instincts, the more satisfaction you will feel.

The Flower Vault is a photographic journal of the blooms seen throughout the book. This section is organized in two ways: first, by color, and second, by season, helping take the guesswork out of when a flower is in bloom.

The last thing I will leave you with is this: It's just flowers. I mentioned this earlier and it bears repeating. It's. Just. Flowers. Yes, they are living art. Yes, they smell great. Yes, to appreciate their fleeting beauty we must learn to stay in the present. Yes, my loves, flowers are amazing. You know what flowers are not? Painful. No, flowers should not cause you to feel hurt or bad about yourself. Flowers will never diminish your light or ask you to sacrifice the best parts of yourself. Nothing and no one should have that much power. It's just flowers.

Love,

Kristen

P.S. Oh, and one more thing . . . I repeat myself. A lot. It's on purpose. I want this information to stick. Just think of me as the best friend you didn't know you needed, never wanted, but are thrilled to have.

Part I

A FLORAL FOUNDATION

---

*W*hether you are new to floristry or have been at it long enough to see carnations come in and out of fashion more often than the mullet, A Floral Foundation is an excellent place to build your vocabulary and prime yourself for the floral journey ahead.

THE TEN FLORAL COMMANDMENTS

1. **There are no rules when it comes to floral design.** I say this to encourage you to think outside the box—including with the designs in this book. I want to empower you to find and nurture your own creative style.

2. **Substitutions are okay!** While it is ideal to have all the same elements shown in each recipe, it is not a requirement. It is not imperative to have the exact stem counts or exact types of flowers listed for every arrangement. Adjusting the stem counts to fit your needs is more than acceptable. Your energy is better spent focusing on the colors within the piece. Substituting a pink rose for a pink peony is a great idea. Substituting a pink rose for a pink hamster? Not so much.

3. **We love a triangle.** Throughout this book, I will ask you to create small triangles (and some other geometric shapes) in the arrangements—and that is on purpose. Triangles provide balance and clarity to an otherwise busy design concept. I've thrown in a few diagrams to help you out, and once you see triangles in floral arrangements, you will not be able to unsee them.

4. **Foliage is not filler.** For our purposes, we will never use greenery or foliage for the sole purpose of making a bouquet or an arrangement look bigger. No flower or leaf is without its purpose. Every element has been selected to support the overall design shape, color, and/or depth of the piece.

5. **Look for the oddballs.** In every bunch of blooms there are always one or two stems that stand out, whether for their unusual beauty or uncommon shape. Do not discount the weirdos. The addition of peculiar elements can easily make a mundane piece stand out—in a good way.

6. **Flowers don't last—and they're not supposed to.** As with all living things, flowers grow, bloom, thrive, and fade away. Use their fleeting beauty as a tether to stay present. Love them while they are here because in the blink of an eye they will be gone.

7. **Rotate, rotate, rotate!** The floral design recipes in this book mostly address the side of the arrangement that faces you. Unless you are doing a one-sided arrangement where the back is not visible, *always* rotate your arrangement to design the other side before moving on to the next step. I am not going to mention this in the floral design recipes. So, it will be up to you to remember it.

8. **Take ownership.** So often my students are curious to know why their pieces don't look exactly like the example. I will tell you the same thing I tell them: You are not a photocopy machine. The floral design recipes are not scientific equations. Use them for guidance and direction. Variety is welcomed and celebrated here.

9. **Be self-indulgent.** This book is a gateway for you to take care of yourself through the beauty of flowers. Take your time! I repeat: Take. Your. Tiiiiiiiiiiiiiiimmmmmmmmeeee. We are going to explore a lot of stunning blooms, make bewitching arrangements, and play with alluring colors. Give them (and yourself) unencumbered attention by limiting pesky distractions.

10. **You deserve flowers.** Oh yes you do. Tell that voice in your head that heard "you deserve flowers" and answered with "no, I don't" to sit down.

TOOLS
AND SUPPLIES

*E*very designer needs a set of good tools they can rely on. Here is a list of tools every florist should have in their kit, purse, fanny pack, and/or glove compartment.

(1) Bind wire: Bind wire is a type of floral wire covered in a waterproof fiber. Durable and lightweight, it is my go-to wire choice when making wreaths and flower crowns. The texture easily camouflages mechanics and blends beautifully into any floral piece.

(2) Bouquet tape: This self-adhering paper tape (also known as stem wrap) becomes tacky when stretched. It is ideal for securing bouquets and boutonnieres. With a firm and controlled hand, wrap the stems with the tape, gently tugging the tape as you work. The bouquet tape should stick to itself. When you're finished, simply tear or cut the tape in the desired spot and use a beautiful ribbon to conceal it.

(3) Chicken wire: If you have a choice between the coated and uncoated versions of chicken wire, go with coated. My hands are just two leather bags with a bad manicure and even they don't like uncoated chicken wire. Chicken wire is light enough to be molded into virtually any shape, yet sturdy enough to hold many stems in place. Chicken wire is paramount in designing architectural floral displays.

(4) Crafting scissors: A sturdy pair of everyday scissors for cutting and trimming a variety of items, including floral tape and kraft paper.

(5) Fabric/ribbon scissors: Different than a household or crafting scissor, fabric shears are specifically engineered to snip and clip textiles with surgical precision.

(6) Floral adhesive: Similar to rubber cement, floral adhesive is a quick-drying solution if you need an alternative to taping or wiring flowers into a display. It is great for making flower crowns, composite bouquets, and corsages. I prefer the clear version, as it is easier to hide its appearance. Use conservatively. Just a dab will do!

(7) Floral clippers: These are shears specifically engineered for cutting stems. Your relationship with your clippers might be the most important relationship you can have with a floral tool. A good pair will make your life easy while a bad pair can leave you questioning every single life choice you have made since the age of twelve! Some clippers have curved blades, while others are straight and serrated. You may need to explore a few different styles before you find what works best for you.

(8) Floral pins: These sharp little guys can be used to secure a ribbon to a bouquet or a boutonniere to a lapel. Available in a wide range of colors and lengths, floral pins are an absolute must-have.

Floral cooler: A floral cooler, if you have one, is an amazing resource to keep your blooms at their freshest. I do not have a floral cooler, but I do have a refrigerator! Placing your blooms in your refrigerator is another way to keep them looking great for a short amount of time (no longer than forty-eight hours).

But what about . . .

. . . **floral foam?** There is none. I'm trying to quit.

. . . **flower food?** I don't use it. Never saw a difference.

(9) Floral/pin frogs: Most of the floral arrangements in this text require the use of a floral frog, sometimes called a pin frog. This foundational tool can be composed of finely tapered needles, ceramic, glass, or a series of metal hooks. No matter what they're made of, floral frogs are a reliable support for architectural floral displays. Secure your frog by placing a few pieces of floral putty underneath its base. In a clean and dry vase, carefully press the frog into the bottom of the vessel and give a slight twist to secure.

(10) Floral putty: Floral putty is a semipermanent waterproof adhesive. Available in white or green, its moldable, clay-like form can be used to attach all sorts of unusual things together, like a floral frog to the inside of a vase or a pair of slippers onto a wall.

(11) Floral wire: Floral wire is great for reinforcing stems, building floral chandeliers, and much more. It is malleable and durable. For best results, use wire cutters when trimming floral wire.

(12) Protective gloves: Always wear protective floral or gardening gloves to guard your hands from potential allergens and other irritants. Oh, and wash your hands when you're done.

(13) Waterproof floral tape: Use waterproof floral tape only on clean, dry surfaces. If the tape gets wet, it will not work as well. I prefer the quarter-inch-wide green variety for its thinness and durability. Floral tape is used for building tape grids, strapping in a chicken wire pillow, and as an extra layer of support when wrapping bouquets. Use crafting scissors to cut it or rip it apart with your hands.

(14) Wire cutters: Florists use wire cutters for snipping floral and chicken wire. If you are able, procure a spring-loaded pair with a rubber handle to make all that snipping much more tolerable. This is crucial if you have the dainty wrists of a fifteenth-century French dauphin, like I do.

(15) Zip ties: These are great for securely attaching a host of floral elements (large branches, silk flowers, or stems) to surfaces like floral cages, watering cones, and floral hoop frames. These plastic fasteners come in a variety of lengths and colors, including green and black. Floral designers also use them to attach chicken wire to a frame or for building floral installations.

FLORALS 101

WAIT. STOP. READ THIS.

If you are here, you are probably looking to learn something new about floral design. Or maybe you just came for the pretty pictures. Either way, I love that for you. There is something uniquely satisfying about taking initiative to seek out new information. Being self-taught has many advantages. The upside is the freedom to view design through a lens that is not complicated by another person's opinion. Having the space to explore and test a variety of styles and techniques without the fear of a failing grade (or worse, the stink-eye from a colleague . . . or even worse, the cold shoulder from a crush) was paramount to my success. Learning in this unconventional way strengthened my connection to my inner authority, helping me to trust myself as a designer. Which, upon reflection, is way more important than what some random hottie working the front desk at the gym thinks about me.

The downside of being self-taught is that I made a lot of mistakes and spent a lot of time patching up amateurish work. I struggled. A lot. I spent way too much time lamenting over how I was going to bring the intention behind each design to life and not enough time enjoying the creative process.

Florals 101 is devoted to expanding your floral-design vocabulary and sharing my best tips and tricks. My hope is that you will bypass the many years I spent learning things the messy way. Think of this as an accelerated education. Feel free to take anything you learn here and adapt it. Then make it better. The first floral commandment demands it.

Asymmetry: When it comes to the shape of a design, asymmetry most resembles forms found in nature. Imagine an uneven stream of sunlight shining a bit brighter on one side of an arrangement than the other. This would give some blooms more height than others. Asymmetry makes an arrangement look architectural and feel alive, as if it were plucked from the garden floor.

Bouquets: Of all the pieces to create, bouquets are my favorite. There is something so personal about making something for someone else to hold. The first tip: A tight, constricting grip will produce a bouquet that looks choked. A firm yet flexible grip gives you the freedom to edit your work without the fear of it all falling apart.

Second, when making a bouquet, viewing it from different angles provides perspective. Look at it first from eye level. Next, hold the arrangement down near your navel while you look at it from above. Then rotate the bouquet so you can examine the back and sides.

Finally, always secure the arrangement with bouquet tape and trim the stems until even. Once trimmed, immediately place it in a vase of cold water until ready to use. Dry off the stems before adding any ribbon or wrappings.

Chicken wire pillow: Practically every design in this book has some sort of armature inside the vase to support the piece. None is more prevalent than the chicken wire pillow. Here is how to make one: Gently scrunch up a section of chicken wire until it becomes a loosely round shape—not squished tight like a ball of aluminum foil but hollow and airy. Refine the shape in your hands until it fits snugly into your vessel. Use a strip of waterproof floral tape to strap it into your vase or pot.

Cleaning your vase: No really, dirt and bacteria can severely shorten the vase life of a flower arrangement. Keeping your vases squeaky clean helps keep your blooms looking fresh.

Creating a cloud: Usually done at the beginning stages of building a floral display. I often use the word "cloud" as a cue for you to create a fluffy amorphous shape out of flowers.

Crosscutting: This technique supports hydration for hardy stems. To crosscut, use your floral clippers to trim the stems at a 45-degree angle, then make a vertical cut up the center of the stem. Rotate the stem 90 degrees to make a second vertical cut up the center of the stem. The cuts on the bottom of the stem should resemble an *X* or +.

Dried flowers: Though most dried flowers need little care, some are brittle and can shed like a cheap faux fur coat. Spray them with a bit of hairspray to keep them in check.

Facing front: When positioning blooms to face front or sit low and drape over the lip of the vase you'll need to insert the stems almost horizontally into your vessel, so the flower's head rests on the lip of your vessel. This requires vigilance about the water level in your vase. For best results, use stems that already have a natural curve to them, so they can reach the water below for hydration.

Floating: To "float" means to position a stem so the bloom sits a few (one to three) inches away from the rest of the arrangement. Floating is a simple way to enhance the shape or add color or depth to a piece without making it feel overly stuffed.

Floral tape grid: A tape grid offers support when designing an architectural piece. Start by laying several lines of floral tape across the mouth of the vessel in parallel, vertical rows, spaced evenly apart. Then cross the vertical strips by laying the same number of lines horizontally. Fold all strips over the edge of the vase and press them down firmly. For extra support, add a tape ring, a long continuous piece of floral tape wrapped around the circumference of the vase to hold down the ends of the grid.

Floral tape strap: A floral tape strap is a necessity when using a chicken wire pillow. The tape strap prevents the chicken wire from shifting in the vase. Trim a strip of waterproof floral tape a little longer than the diameter of the vase's mouth. Attach one end of the tape to one side of the vase, stretch it across the top, and attach to the opposite side. Use two additional pieces of floral tape to secure the strap to the vase. If you are feeling cautious, you can do a double tape strap or add a tape ring.

Floral triage: Some flowers require extra attention when conditioning, especially those that wilt, won't open up, or bend under the weight of their heads.

- **Paper collars:** A paper collar helps support stems with heavy heads. It can also help blooms that are prematurely opening to stay closed longer. Fold or trim a large piece of recyclable paper into a triangle. Gently wrap a single bloom with the paper to form a collar just below its head. Use a piece of tape to fasten the paper. Trim and hydrate the freshly cut stems in four to six inches of very warm water. Immediately place them in a floral cooler or refrigerated area for a minimum of twelve hours. When placed in a cooler, flowers constrict, locking in the absorbed warm water for prolonged hydration. Do not leave the paper collar on for more than thirty-six hours.

- **Straws:** Before throwing unused plastic straws in the trash, consider putting them to good use. Slide thin-stemmed blooms such as *Scabiosa* or *Gerbera* into the straws to keep flowers looking alert.

- **Warm water:** Warm—not hot—water is great for forcing tight blooms to open quickly. It is also great for reviving wilting blooms and hydrating woody-stemmed flora. Dunking the head of a tightly closed bud in a bath of warm water helps dissolve the sticky sap covering the sepals and outer petals, allowing the bud to bloom into a ruffled fantasy. If the bud is immature, however, this method will not work as well. You can tell buds are mature when they have taken on the intended color of the flower, while immature buds remain mostly green.

Flower conditioning: Whether or not to condition flowers is a bit of a hot topic among florists. I have worked with some designers who don't condition at all. They simply plop the fresh stems into a bucket of water and don't revisit them until it is time to design. Other designers are precious with the flowers, spending hours meticulously cleaning each stem to perfection. I fall somewhere in the middle. Conditioning flowers gives you the best chance at getting the most out of your investment.

Removing excessive foliage or lateral blooms that will never mature, trimming the ends of the stems, and hydrating your fresh flowers in clean water increases the likelihood that the blooms will last longer.

Each of the floral-design recipes in this book has a section on flower conditioning called "Flower Prep," which is just a hip way of saying it.

Foliage: Removing foliage from a stem helps conserve the already limited energy of a cut flower and prevents bacteria from growing in the water. Always remove any leaves from a stem that will be submerged in water.

Hydration: Don't skip this one. Skipping out on hydrating your flowers is as senseless as trying to make ice cream in the oven. It is ideal to hydrate each type of stem in a different vessel, but I'd say it's okay to hydrate like stems with like stems (that is, woody stems can hydrate together, fibrous stems with other fibrous stems, and so on). There are two key considerations that can make a difference when hydrating your stems:

- **Water levels:** Most stems do well in shallow water. Woody stems enjoy a restorative plunge in deep water. In each floral design recipe, you will see a suggestion for the amount of water to hydrate the flowers in.

- **Temperature:** In general, cold water is standard. However, some flowers do well in tepid water while others need warm water to encourage proper hydration. In each recipe, the ideal temperature for each type of flower is written out.

Leaking stems: Some flowers (like *Narcissus*, hyacinths, poinsettias, milkweed, tweedia, and euphorbia and all her cousins) leak a milky or clear fluid after being cut. Some of this fluid is toxic and when mixed with other flowers can accelerate deterioration. For these kinds of blooms, measure twice and cut once. Place the cut stems in four to six inches of warm water until the leaking has ceased (around fifteen minutes). Blot the ends of stems or any leaking points until dry.

Mechanics: "Mechanics" refers to anything added to the frame, base, or vessel to help make an arrangement. This includes chicken wire, floral frogs, and tape grids. As the design of each piece progresses, it is important to *hide the mechanics* from nosy neighbors trying to decipher your design secrets. If they want to know that badly, tell them to get a copy of this book.

Placement: I know, I know, this looks like geometry. That's because it is . . . I think. There are a lot of parts of an arrangement to cover, so the instructions will often point you to a specific area to place a stem.

Each arrangement is divided into **five vertical sections:** left, left of center, center, right of center, and right; and **three horizontal sections:** low, medium, and tall.

Each bouquet is divided into **nine sections (like a sudoku puzzle):** upper left, upper center, upper right, middle left, middle center, middle right, lower left, lower center, and lower right.

Reflexing: There is no point to turning the outer petals of a flower inside out other than to give them an otherworldly appearance. This does not work for every flower; the easiest to reflex are roses, tulips, and lisianthus. Be aware that stiff, tight flowers will most likely tear if reflexed too early. Wait for the blooms to loosen and soften before gently using your thumb and forefinger to flip the petals inside out.

Reuse the itty bitties: Use any leftovers or stems that are too small for an arrangement or other floral projects. Consider using unused blooms to make an arrangement in a bud vase for the side of your bed or a hanging posy for the bathroom.

Ribbon: If you plan to add a flowing ribbon to a bouquet, wait to add it until the last possible moment before its presentation (and only after the stems have been thoroughly dried off). I prefer 1.5- or 2-inch satin ribbons to wrap the stems of my bouquets. Here's how:

1. At the back of the bouquet, hold one end of the ribbon. Wrap the stems using the ribbon, making sure to cover any visible bouquet tape.

2. Trim the ribbon and fold the raw edge down. Use two or three small floral pins to secure the ribbon to the stems. Be sure to angle the pins into the heart of the stems so the sharp ends do not poke out.

3. Use a bow or a slipknot to attach the ribbon around the trunk of your bouquet. Add a small floral pin to secure the ribbon to the bouquet.

Sourcing fresh flowers: Buy local if you can! The flowers seen in this text were exclusively grown in the USA. Many were grown and harvested in the Pacific Northwest, thanks to the incredible farms, florists, and growing community at the Seattle Wholesale Growers Market. Supporting your local farmers is good for the environment and economy. Head to **The Flower Vault** on page 261 for more information.

Spiraling stems: Arranging stems in a sort of twisted fashion makes it easy to thread and remove blooms from a bouquet as you're working on it.

1. Crisscross two stems to make an *X* shape.

2. Choose one of your stems in the *X* as the anchor for your spiral. Then, adding one at a time, place additional stems into your bouquet, following the line and direction of your anchor stem. If the anchor stem is inserted from the right side of the bouquet, add all proceeding stems from the right.

3. Do not change directions. This will create weak points in the bouquet resulting in bent or broken stems.

Threading: Threading is a technique often used when designing a bouquet. It allows you to add flowers to any section of the piece without disrupting your progress. When holding the arranged bouquet, carefully loosen your grip. Maintaining your slackened grip, gently slide any additional stems into the trunk of the bouquet from the top. With each additional stem, you will begin to feel your grip tighten as the width of the trunk increases. When you're done, tighten your grip to its original tension and continue working.

On vases

Each recipe includes a section on how to prepare your vase for the arrangement. Vases are an important aesthetic element of any arrangement, as they emphasize the shape and communicate intention.

There is no expectation for you to match the vases from the book, but if you decide to size up or down, be sure to adjust the mechanics and stem counts (by 15 to 20 percent for each size up or down) to coordinate with the vase you select.

BTW: You should know that I have a serious shopping problem when it comes to vases. I don't know how it happens, but whenever I go shopping, I somehow end up coming back with a vase . . . or six. There are so many different drool-worthy shapes and sizes to play with. From rounded bubble-shaped vases and quaint footed ceramic bowls to tall glittering flutes of mercury glass; I love them all. There isn't a vase that I don't love. Wait! I take that back. If I see one more mason jar with a burlap bow . . . well, let's just say there would not be enough looking-up-while-shaking-a-fist-to-the-sky GIFs to capture my disdain. Other than that; I am totally open to vases of all shapes and sizes.

Trimming: When conditioning your blooms, trimming the stems on a 45-degree angle increases the surface area a stem has available to take in water. For woody stems, see Crosscutting on page 21.

Vase life: Vase life refers to how long a cut flower arrangement will survive once in the vase. Your creations should last anywhere from three to five days, depending on the freshness of the blooms and the conditions of the room they are displayed in. Here are a few ways to help maximize an arrangement's vase life:

◊ Use a clean vase.

◊ Keep the water fresh.

◊ Keep flowers away from heaters and direct sunlight.

◊ Remove dying blooms.

Water: Use filtered or distilled water whenever possible to support the longevity of your arrangement. Otherwise, cool tap water is an acceptable alternative.

Waterproofing: When designing in a vase that is not watertight, you must add a liner. The quickest and easiest solution is to put a smaller waterproof vase of a similar shape inside the leaky vase. For a vase of an unusual shape, such as an urn, I recommend a moldable waterproof material like floral foil. Press the foil into the inside of the vase until it takes on the shape of the full vessel. Make sure there are no cracks or hidden holes in the liner. Use your scissors to trim the foil so the edges slightly fold over the lip of the vase. Add a floral tape strap to secure the foil in place. Any additional mechanics, such as chicken wire or floral frogs, must be added *after* the liner is secure.

HOW TO USE THIS BOOK

*A*s you make your way through this text, you may notice that there is more to do than look at the pretty pictures. Yes, my flower friends, this book also includes floral-design recipes to guide you through each step needed to make masterpieces of your own. As you read through each floral-design recipe, you will notice the following:

Difficulty level: There are three levels of difficulty for the arrangements in this book: Beginner, Advanced, Expert.

Season: This is when most of the ingredients for the arrangement should become available. This may be different depending on your location. It is best to check in with your local growers and flower suppliers regarding availability.

Mood: Flowers can transform your life. If you are looking to create something cheerful or dramatic, let the mood label point you towards the right piece.

Color palette: This is a visual snapshot of the notable hues seen in the display.

Ingredients: This is a list of all the flowers used in the design. Sourcing the exact same ingredients may not be an option depending on where you live and what your local market is able to source. At your discretion, feel free to make substitutions based on color, texture, or your own design flair.

Flower prep: Here you will find helpful tips on how to condition your blooms before arranging.

Vase prep: These are instructions on how to prepare your vase for different styles of floral design. The one constant is to always, always, always clean and dry your vase before adding fresh flowers to it.

Each floral design recipe is then broken down into three key elements: Shape, Color, and Depth. All include step-by-step instructions.

CRAFTING A COLOR STORY

*N*ews flash: Anybody can stick flowers into a brick of floral foam and call it an arrangement. Gorgeous, show-stopping floral design, however, is challenging. It is a discipline that challenges us to balance individualism and creativity on the tip of Mother Nature's finger. With all the elements of an arrangement to consider, it is easy to become overwhelmed by the excess of options.

Choosing a color palette is one of the vast and varied choices you'll need to make. Before diving into the floral design recipes, let's take a moment to deepen our understanding of color.

In nurturing your relationship with color, you will come to understand the difference between blue, kind-of-blue, and blue-ish. Let us begin with one simple rule: Color is not flat.

1. **Identify your intention.** Name it. Do you want the piece to feel wild or demure? Sassy or unassuming? Once the intention has been identified, think of each shade you choose as a thread pulled from the rainbow. The color story of an arrangement is a collection of individual threads, taut and vibrating, woven together with your intention to create one clearly defined idea.

It can be as simple as "I want to create something that feels whimsical" or as complicated as "I want to create something that represents the time I spent pretending to be a nun in San Francisco in 1993." While the latter does sound rather joyful, for time's sake, let's explore the whimsical option.

2. **Paint your narrative.** Start by pondering what *whimsical* means to you. When I think of *whimsical,* I am reminded of the thrill of eating pink-and-blue cotton candy at the Michigan State Fair as a child. I think of a giant pastel

option A

bouquet of balloons teasing adventurous children like myself with promises of flight. I think of the green grounds flattened under the excitement of its patrons. Words like *buoyant*, *bendy*, and *effervescent* swim to the front of my mind.

3. **Build your color palette.** The broad strokes of my palette include hues of pink, blue, and green with a variety of pastels and potentially indigo. What are your colors? Write them down.

Let's dream up two color palettes to choose from. Above, you'll see that option A is composed of soft shades of pastel that work effortlessly together. On the next page, you'll see that option B, while mostly pastel, includes millennium blue—a darker shade of indigo. To assess, let's revisit our intention: *whimsical*, which brought up the descriptive words *buoyant*, *bendy*, and *effervescent*. Option A, with its soft hues of Tsumugi pink, ruddy blue, sweet cream, buttermilk, lavender, and arctic lime, is weightless and playful. The color palette has been established.

option B

4. **Clarify your design.** Make easy work of this by creating a list of a few "shoulds" and "should nots" to set boundaries to guide the work. Take a peek at my lists below and then give it a whirl!

THE DESIGN SHOULD . . .	THE DESIGN SHOULD NOT . . .
Have elements of height	Be condensed or flat
Have negative space	Be overstuffed with flowers
Have a unique shape	Be symmetrical in shape
Have movement	Be stiff
Have an explosive energy	Be restrained

5. **Let it all out.** You don't have to hold back the energy brewing inside of you any longer. To craft a color story is to pour memories, feelings, moods, backstory, and colors into your arrangement. Make what was once an intangible spark of creativity into a tangible work of art. The creative energy you have gifted to your arrangements is the key difference between acceptable and *exceptional* floral design.

Now that you know and now that I know that you know that I know you know, only one question remains . . .

What will *your* color story be?

FLOWERS
ARE SELF-CARE

*W*hat is self-care? How do you define it? How do you find that perfect combination of doing something or nothing to charge your emotional battery? Self-care can be as simple as chomping on a stick of bubblegum or as trying as competing in a triathlon. It might simply be sitting in silence. While the definition of self-care varies based on personal preference, one thing is universally clear: **Self-care is a necessity.** Like water. And just like water, the more you hydrate, the better you will feel. Consistently offering yourself time for self-care (and the love and attention you deserve) is equally as important as the act of self-care itself.

Consider what self-care looks like for you. What fills you up, calms you down, brings you peace of mind? What kinds of practices would you like to adopt? How can you generate peace, care, and happiness from within?

I will be the first to admit life is complicated. Adulting is hard. If you are anything like me, putting yourself and your needs last might be your default, leaving you with no energy to maintain a healthy relationship with the person that needs you the most: *yourself.*

Happiness comes from within. Self-care nurtures happiness.

I repeat: *Happiness comes from within. Self-care nurtures happiness.* Like a bacon-wrapped date, one cannot exist without the other. They are meant to be together.

Plus, looking externally for happiness is not sustainable or satisfying and is about as wise as bleaching your hair without a toner. Don't ask me how I know . . . (Okay, I'll bite. I tried it once and my hair was so orange I ended up looking like Carrot Top's gay cousin, Velveeta!)

YOUR FLOWER STORY

*I*f you have not thrown this book across the room out of frustration because I have yet to teach you about flowers, I would like to (a) thank you, because I worked really hard on it and to dent this beautiful cover would be so messed up and (b) invite you to use this book as the first step in what I hope will be many joy-filled steps towards improving your relationship with yourself.

To care for yourself is to show yourself love > Love heals wounds old and new > To love flowers is to love nature > Nature also fosters healing; therefore, flowers are *what*? Let's say it together: **FLOWERS ARE SELF-CARE!**

Here are three ways working with flowers can improve your relationship with yourself:

1. Floral design reclaims your time. Taking as little as five minutes a day to be with flowers sends an internal memo to your brain that you are worth taking time for. The notion that caring for yourself is somehow inconsiderate is a garbage narrative passed down to diminish the positives of being self-indulgent. It is time to recognize your worth. So, when it comes to your self-care, normalize being self-indulgent. Acknowledge what the rest of us already know about you: You are worth the time.

2. Floral design can be physiologically therapeutic. Channeling energy into a creative project has been said to improve brain function and mental health. The sensory stimulation is not to be overlooked either. Floral design is exhausting—the good kind of exhausting that accompanies achievement. Sort of like when you work out or cook Thanksgiving dinner all by yourself. These kinds of achievements can lead to an increase of serotonin and dopamine in the body. Floral design is a mental, physical, and creative challenge *and* an excellent way to purge your psyche of negativity so you can channel your energy into creating something beautiful.

3. Floral design helps build self-confidence.

Let's face it, being really good at something is empowering and can make you feel like a badass. It may start out a bit rocky, and for that, I encourage you to stick with it. The more you practice the better you will get. More practice = more confidence. Just like more cheese = more yummy. It's simple math!

Despite what George and Ira had to say about it, these days the livin' *ain't* easy. We've all got plenty of material to beat ourselves down with. Let's put an end to that, shall we?

From here on out, floral design is your shield against negative self-talk, online trolls, and shady waiters who don't bring you extra pickles. Keep practicing your craft. As your expertise grows, so will your self-confidence. In time, you will come to realize you no longer need to shield yourself from you, because you have nothing to prove. You never did.

My hope is that working with flowers helps you recognize that your gifts and creativity are a strength. Your creations are an extension of you. Let the floral displays you create from this tome be a living reminder that you—yes, YOU!—are enough.

Part II

A RAINBOW OF ARRANGEMENTS

Red

FALU

I've always been fascinated by flowers that mimic other forms seen in nature. *Allium siculum,* with their long stems that rise into umbrella-shaped domes, remind me of a visit I took to the Georgia Aquarium in Atlanta where I witnessed hundreds of jellyfish hypnotically pulsing in the abyss. Jellyfish are known to have high reproductive rates, which can result in a large population increase in a short period of time. Coincidentally, this phenomenon is called a "bloom." Inspired by the ethereal form of these aquatic angels, this arrangement celebrates the resilience, beauty, and danger of such hypnotic creatures.

INGREDIENTS

14 STEMS
ALLIUM SICULUM
'SUMMER BELLS'

12 STEMS
GARDEN ROSE
'GRAND JUBILEE'

COLOR PALETTE

RASPBERRY   FALU RED   CARMINE

45

Flower Prep

ALLIUM

Allium are cousins to leeks and onions and do not require deep water to thrive. Trim on a 45-degree angle and hydrate in cold water.

4–6"
COLD

Pro tip

Don't worry, that hard to locate body odor smell is not you! It's the flowers! *Allium* can have a slight oniony scent. Change the water often with fresh, cold water to reduce the smell.

GARDEN ROSE

Remove all thorns and foliage from the garden roses. Pick out the longest stem and place it in a vase of tepid water off to the side. We'll use this tall guy later. Once cleaned, trim on a 45-degree angle and hydrate in warm water.

DEEP
WARM

Vase Prep

Create a tape grid on a tall cylindrical vase. Space the lines of the tape grid about half an inch apart. The close spacing provides support for tall, slender stems. Fill the vase three-quarters of the way with cold water.

Shape and Color

1. Trim 7 stems of *Allium* and place them low, so they hang over the lip of the vase, obscuring the tape grid. Place the tallest of these stems to the right of center to create asymmetry.

2. Set aside the tallest garden rose stem to use later. Trim 2 garden rose stems and place them low, floating just above the *Allium:* Add 1 stem to the front left side of the vase, then rotate the arrangement and repeat this placement on the backside.

3. Start to the right of center of the tape grid and gradually add 6 *Allium* stems to create a shape that looks as though the flowers are exploding outward from the middle of the arrangement like a firework, reaching out in all directions: left, right, up and out, back, front. These stems should range in length from medium to tall.

4. Trim 1 final *Allium* stem so it is taller than the others and place it to reach out and up from the left, bringing asymmetry to the shape.

Depth

5. Trim 1 short red garden rose stem and place it low, on the right side of the vase, mirroring the position of the rose placed in step 2. Rotate the vase and repeat this placement on the backside. Once placed, rotate the vase to face front again.

6. Starting just above the lowest roses, place a cluster of 7 more roses of medium length to stretch out and away from the left side of the arrangement. This creates a deliciously dark red shadow.

7. Lastly, for a bit of drama, add the tall garden rose set aside earlier to reach up and out from the right side of the arrangement.

Remember, your time in this space is for no one other than you. It's okay to take a five-minute break. Or a one-hour break. You can even take a nap! The only obligation is that you use this creative space to address the needs of the most important person in your life: YOU.

A RAINBOW OF ARRANGEMENTS

MERLOT

*P*eonies. We all love them. Lusciously ruffled in a charming shade of cherry red, the 'Red Charm' peony delights when paired with shades of merlot and pale pink. Selected for their minimal size and buoyancy, I've added *Astrantia* and Butterfly Ranunculus to enhance this treasured bloom. Plus, let's not kid ourselves: There is no way a flower as fabulous as a peony is going to easily fade into the background. It is better to let it shine.

INGREDIENTS

5 STEMS PEONY 'RED CHARM'	7 STEMS *ASTRANTIA MAJOR* 'GILL RICHARDSON'	9 STEMS BUTTERFLY RANUNCULUS 'ARIADNE'

COLOR PALETTE

CHERRY RED	MERLOT	PALE PINK

TOOLS

BOUQUET TAPE
FLORAL CLIPPERS
PROTECTIVE GLOVES
DECORATIVE RIBBON (OPTIONAL)
FABRIC SCISSORS (OPTIONAL)

Flower Prep

Carefully remove all foliage from the stems. Trim on a 45-degree angle and hydrate in cool water.

4–6"
COOL

Shape

1. Aiming for an asymmetric shape, loosely gather 4 stems of the peony to form a cloud. Create a focal point by placing the fifth and final stem on the right side of the bouquet, so it floats away from the peony cloud.

Color

2. Begin by threading 1 stem of *Astrantia* into the center of the bouquet so it slightly floats above the peonies (see Threading on page 29).

3. Create a cluster of *Astrantia* with the remaining 6 stems, placing them so they fan out towards the upper left side of the bouquet. The intoxicating merlot shade of these *Astrantia* enriches the color palette without making the piece feel heavy.

Hey you, you're almost done. Time to warm up those gams for a happy dance.

Depth

4. Soften the form of the bouquet by dispersing 8 stems of Butterfly Ranunculus throughout the bouquet. Ensure the peonies remain visible by gathering the Butterfly Ranunculus near the perimeter of the bouquet. Clustering soft-hued flowers helps maximize their impact in a layered arrangement.

5. To create visual interest, position the final stem of Butterfly Ranunculus to reach out from the lower right corner.

6. Finish by securing the stems with bouquet tape. Trim the stems evenly. Hydrate in a vase of cold water until ready to use.

Optional

Add a ribbon of your choice. Use fabric scissors to trim the ends of the ribbon at a 45-degree angle (see Ribbon on page 28).

HOLLY

A pep talk from a loved one is a great source of momentary comfort. If you are looking for glowing confidence all day, every day, become your own hype man. You are all you will ever need to shine from within.

DIFFICULTY LEVEL
beginner

SEASON
winter

MOOD
festive

HOLLY

Whether you are celebrating the holidays or trying to escape them, nothing says "I am ready to dunk my face in a punchbowl full of eggnog" quite like a festive floral arrangement. Stuffed with double petal poinsettias and velvety 'Black Baccara' roses, this arrangement is a decadent way to celebrate how masterfully you navigated everything that has been thrown at you over the past year. You're still here. You've made it. Time to pop the bubbly and make something special for yourself. No one is more deserving than you.

INGREDIENTS

15 STEMS POINSETTIA
'WINTER ROSE'

15 STEMS ROSE
'BLACK BACCARA'

COLOR PALETTE

HOLLY   VERMONT GREEN   CRANBERRY SAUCE

Flower Prep

POINSETTIA

Wear gloves when handling the poinsettia stems. This plant leaks a milky fluid when cut or damaged (see leaking stems on page 25). Do not trim the ends until you are ready to place into the arrangement. Keep the stems in room temperature water until you are ready for them.

 4–6"
ROOM TEMP

ROSE

Remove all thorns and foliage from the rose stems. Trim on a 45-degree angle and hydrate in warm water.

 DEEP
WARM

Vase Prep

In a large oblong bowl, add a pillow of chicken wire. Use a floral tape strap to secure the pillow in the vase.

Shape

1. Starting low, place 11 poinsettia stems in the vase to create a fluffy, oblong shape.

2. Starting from the left of center, add the remaining 4 poinsettia stems to create an asymmetric shape that branches up and out towards the left.

Warning! This part of the process requires moving the arrangement to and from the sink. Once in water, cut poinsettia stems will begin to leak and the water will need to be drained.

3. Let the leaky poinsettia stems drain for 10 to 15 minutes, or until done leaking. Hold your vessel under a faucet and run a fresh batch of water directly into the vase until the cloudy water becomes clear. Carefully remove the vase from the sink and dry off the exterior.

Color

4. Set aside 4 of the taller rose stems to use later. Add the remaining 11 roses to the lowest parts of your arrangement, filling in any open gaps or spaces near the lip, obscuring any visible mechanics.

Depth

5. On the right side of the arrangement, add your 4 reserved roses to mirror the spray of poinsettias on the left.

To all of you, I send my warmest and most sincere thanks. You are loved. Happy Holidays.

Love, Kristen

DIFFICULTY LEVEL
advanced

SEASON
autumn

MOOD
romantic

HEROINE

With the fire of Lizzie Bennet, the passion of Janie Crawford, and the undying beauty of Alice Walker's Celie, this piece celebrates the great literary heroines of our time. Layered in alluring shades of black cherry and onyx, this loving color story turns even the most hardened of hearts to putty. Romantic and a bit sassy, it is a historical romance novel reborn as a floral arrangement.

INGREDIENTS

20 ROSEHIP TIPS
'MAGICAL PEARLS'

8 STEMS
LEUCADENDRON 'EBONY'

6 STEMS ROSE
'ROUGE ROYALE'

20 STEMS *SCABIOSA ATROPURPUREA*
'BLACKBERRY SCOOP'

1 STEM *AGONIS FLEXUOSA*
'JERVIS BAY AFTERDARK'

COLOR PALETTE

| STILETTO RED | BLACK CHERRY | CANDY APPLE | BLACKBERRY | ONYX |

CHICKEN WIRE
FLORAL CLIPPERS
PIN FROG, SMALL
PROTECTIVE GLOVES
WATERPROOF FLORAL TAPE
WIRE CUTTERS

Flower Prep

LEUCADENDRON, ROSEHIPS

Separate any lateral shoots from the main *Leucadendron* stems, with the goal of doubling the number of stems on hand. After dividing up the shoots, you should have a total of 15 to 20 *Leucadendron* stems. Trim the rosehip tips and *Leucadendron* on a 45-degree angle and hydrate in room temperature water.

 4–6"
ROOM TEMP

ROSE

Remove all foliage and thorns from the roses. Trim on a 45-degree angle and hydrate in room temperature water.

 DEEP
ROOM TEMP

SCABIOSA, AGONIS

Remove all foliage and any lateral branching off the main stem of the *Scabiosa*. Remove foliage from the lower part of the *Agonis* stem. Trim the stems at a 45-degree angle and hydrate in 2-4 inches of cold water.

 2–4"
COLD

Vase Prep

In a small vase, add a pin frog and top with a chicken wire pillow. Secure the chicken wire with a floral tape strap. Fill the vase with cold water.

Shape

1. Working from the center of the vase to the outer edges, place 8 cropped rosehip tips in the vase to make a short, tufted shape. Add an additional 3 stems to create height and build out the shape.

2. Use 8 *Leucadendron* stems to fill in the gaps, add density, and slightly widen the shape of your arrangement. Set the shortest of your *Leucadendron* in the center of the vase and work left to right, increasing the height until the tallest stems stretch out from the right side of the vessel.

3. Do the same with the rosehips: Take 9 stems and add to the arrangement in ascending height order, rounding out and softening the asymmetric shape created by the *Leucadendron*.

Color

4. To the left of center, tuck in 1 short rose stem to give a hint of color against the dark *Leucadendron*. As you work with your roses, once the petals are a bit loosened up, reflex the outermost petals for maximum impact (see Reflexing on page 27).

5. Add 5 more roses to the arrangement. Place the tallest stem in the upper left corner and the 4 shorter stems draping out of both sides of the vase.

Depth

6. Like an explosion that arcs from the center of the arrangement outward in every direction, add the 20 *Scabiosa* stems.

7. In the middle of the vase and just to the left of center, place the tall stem of *Agonis*.

Take a moment to reflect on the real-life heroines in your life. This arrangement is dedicated to my heroines: Marsha Sakwa, who showed me the power of language; Vesper Gibbs-Barnes, who showed me the power of leadership; Bianca Dickerson, Jayna Gardner-Grey, and Reina Schackel, who showed me the power of friendship; and my mother, Pauline Griffith, who showed me the power of love.

A RAINBOW OF ARRANGEMENTS

DIFFICULTY LEVEL
advanced

SEASON
winter

MOOD
bold

SCARLET

*S*eeing red? Luckily, this time it's not because your boss keeps calling you Karen even though your name is Miranda. Instead, the red you're seeing is from a spitfire of a bouquet stuffed with lush roses, flirty *Anemones*, and sultry butterfly ranunculus. Oh, and that calm, grounded feeling isn't from spreading a rumor that your boss has head lice. No, no, no, that feeling of calm is from the balance this bouquet has achieved by adding subtle hints of chocolate and matcha. For once, the red you see isn't rage, it's ravishing!

INGREDIENTS

10 STEMS GARDEN ROSE 'MATADOR'

7 STEMS DRIED TEASEL 'FULLER'S TEASEL'

7 STEMS *DAUCUS CAROTA* 'CHOCOLATE LACE'

9 STEMS BUTTERFLY RANUNCULUS 'HADES'

3 STEMS *ANEMONE CORONARIA* 'HIS EXCELLENCY'

COLOR PALETTE

SCARLET · CHOCOLATE · MATCHA · CARDINAL RED · METALLIC NAVY

BOUQUET TAPE
FLORAL CLIPPERS
PROTECTIVE GLOVES
DECORATIVE RIBBON (OPTIONAL)
FABRIC SCISSORS (OPTIONAL)

Flower Prep

GARDEN ROSE

Remove all foliage and thorns
from the roses. Trim on a
45-degree angle and hydrate
in room temperature water.

 DEEP
ROOM TEMP

TEASEL

Set the dried teasels to the side—
no need to hydrate them. Teasel
stems can be prickly with small
thorns. Handle with care.

DAUCUS

Trim the *Daucus* stems
on a 45-degree angle and
hydrate in cold water.

 2–4"
COLD

RANUNCULUS,
ANEMONE

Remove all foliage from the
Ranunculus stems. Trim the
Ranunculus and *Anemone*
stems on a 45-degree angle
and hydrate in cold water.

 4–6"
COLD

Pro tip

Keep quickly blooming *Anemone*
buds closed by storing them in a cool
area, floral cooler, or refrigerator (see
Floral cooler on page 15).

Shape

1. Form the base of your bouquet by gathering 5 garden rose
   stems, creating a petite cluster. Build out the shape by floating
   5 additional stems in front of the cluster: 1 stem in the middle,
   2 facing out to the right, and 2 facing out to the left.

Color

2. Carefully add all 7 teasel stems starting from the center of
   the bouquet and working towards the upper left side. The
   uppermost stem of teasel should reach out a few inches from
   the bouquet, away from the outer left corner.

3. Starting from the right side of the bouquet, thread all
   7 *Daucus* stems evenly throughout the right side of the
   bouquet (see Threading on page 29). Place 1 of the stems on
   the upper right side so it mirrors the position of the tallest
   teasel on the left.

Depth

4. Starting in the middle and working towards the upper and
   lower right corners of the bouquet, add 7 stems of Butterfly
   Ranunculus.

5. Place the final 2 stems so 1 stem reaches out from the lower
   right side and the other reaches out from the upper right side.

6. Form a triangle on the left side of the bouquet with the
   Anemones. Place 2 stems to reach out from the upper left
   corner and 1 stem on the lower left side of the bouquet.

7. Finish by securing the stems with bouquet tape. Trim the
   stems until even.

Optional

Add a ribbon of your choice. Use fabric
scissors to trim the ends of the ribbon at a
45-degree angle (see Ribbon on page 28).

65

GARDEN WONDER

*D*renched in sun-kissed shades of red and gold, this beguiling bouquet sings to the joys of midsummer like an enchanted fairy queen to her Bottom. Vibrant, saturated hues from *Dahlias*, roses, and amaranth work together to clarify the design. Add the bright green *Leycesteria formosa* and winks of pinky lavender *Gomphrena globosa* to create what looks like a flurry of jubilant sprites reveling in a garden of wonders.

INGREDIENTS

10 STEMS *LEYCESTERIA FORMOSA* 'GOLDEN LANTERNS'

3 STEMS *DAHLIA* 'BROWN SUGAR'

5 STEMS *DAHLIA* 'GARDEN WONDER'

6 STEMS GARDEN ROSE 'PIANO FREILAND'

7 STEMS AMARANTH 'HOT BISCUITS'

5 STEMS *GOMPHRENA GLOBOSA* 'QIS PINK'

COLOR PALETTE

| CHARTREUSE | TANGELO | CANDY RED | DIVA RED | SPICY HONEY | PINKY LAVENDER |

TOOLS

BOUQUET TAPE
FLORAL CLIPPERS
PROTECTIVE GLOVES
DECORATIVE RIBBON (OPTIONAL)
FABRIC SCISSORS (OPTIONAL)

Flower Prep

Carefully remove all foliage, thorns, and any laterals branching from the stems of the *Dahlias*, roses, and *Gomphrena*. Remove as much foliage as possible from the amaranth, leaving the foliage closest to the blooms intact.

DAHLIA, GOMPHRENA, AMARANTH

Trim the *Dahlia*, *Gomphrena*, and amaranth stems on a 45-degree angle and hydrate in cold water.

 2–4"
COLD

ROSE

Trim the rose stems on a 45-degree angle and hydrate in room temperature water.

 DEEP
ROOM TEMP

Shape

1. Gather all the *Leycesteria* in your hands to create a loose bush. Create asymmetry by pulling 1 stem out from the top right corner and 1 stem out from the bottom left corner.

Color

2. Bring in a delicious burst of color by adding all 8 *Dahlia* stems (both varieties) and all 6 garden rose stems to the shape created by the *Leycesteria*. Place the stems at different heights by tucking a few deep within the shape while floating other stems farther out. Thread the flowers through the *Leycesteria* so its chartreuse leaves peek through (see Threading on page 29). This pop of color will help break up the intensity of the colorful blooms.

Self-love time

Take a moment to admire your beautiful creation. To have taken time out of your hectic life to create something beautiful for yourself is monumental. It's so beautiful that we could finish here . . . but this book is all about taking it to the next level. So, let's proceed!

Depth

3. Add 3 stems of amaranth to the upper right side of the bouquet. Working on a downward diagonal towards the lower left corner, thread the remaining 4 stems into the bouquet. The final stem should reach out and away from the lower left side of the bouquet.

4. Add 1 stem of *Gomphrena* to the center of the bouquet. Add 3 more stems to the lower right side and 1 stem to the left side. Placing these stems on the periphery of the bouquet allows them to breathe. They should appear as though they are stretching out from the edges of the bunch.

5. Finish by securing the stems with bouquet tape and, if you like, a ribbon. Trim the ends of the stems evenly and place in cold water until ready to use.

Optional

Add a ribbon of your choice. Use fabric scissors to trim the ends of the ribbon at a 45-degree angle (see Ribbon on page 28).

A RAINBOW OF ARRANGEMENTS

Orange

DIFFICULTY LEVEL
beginner

SEASON
summer

MOOD
romantic

DARK CORAL

*C*elosia is an unusual and beautiful flower reminiscent of coral. With crinkles and ripples that skim across the surface of its bloom like gentle waves in a summer breeze, *Celosia* brings the perfect blend of something soft and sculptural to this bouquet. This bouquet is heavily textured with *Dahlias* and three varieties of *Celosia*. The shape and texture, paired with a warm color palette, come together to create a wondrous work of art that looks as though it has been plucked from the crest of an oceanic reef.

INGREDIENTS

4 STEMS
CELOSIA 'BOMBAY FIRE'

4 STEMS
CELOSIA 'SUPERCREST'

12 STEMS
DAHLIA 'A LA MODE'

12 STEMS
CELOSIA 'CELWAY TERRACOTTA'

COLOR PALETTE

RED CLAY SUNSET   GOLDEN CORAL   BRONZED PEACH   DARK CORAL

Flower Prep

CELOSIA

Remove all foliage from the *Celosia* stems. Trim on a 45-degree angle and hydrate in cold water.

4–6"
COLD

DAHLIA

Trim the *Dahlia* stems on a 45-degree angle and hydrate in room temperature water. If necessary, store in a cool area, floral cooler, or refrigerator until ready to use (see Floral cooler on page 15).

6–8"
COLD

Shape

1. Gather all 4 stems of 'Bombay Fire' *Celosia* in your hands to form a cloud. The shape should appear lumpy and uneven.

Color

2. Position 1 stem of 'Supercrest' *Celosia* to reach out from the lower center section of the bouquet.

3. Add the remaining 3 'Supercrest' *Celosia* stems to the top, left, and right edges of the cloud created by the 'Bombay Fire' *Celosia*.

Pro tip

If your wrists and hands are like mine, remember it is okay to take a break. Use bouquet tape to wrap the stems. Then put the bouquet in water to hydrate while you shake out your hands. It's like pressing CTRL+S for flowers.

Depth

4. Add 2 *Dahlia* stems to the center of the bouquet.

5. Use the remaining 10 *Dahlias* to pull the color from the center of the bouquet towards the outer edges. Position a few of the flowers to extend dramatically from the sides of the bouquet.

6. Add all the 'Celway Terracotta' *Celosia* stems to the perimeter of the bouquet, filling in any gaps between the *Dahlias*. Keep most of these stems fairly close to the bouquet so the *Dahlias* are not overshadowed. The *Celosia* should look as though they are peeking curiously from the back of the bouquet.

7. Finish by securing the stems with bouquet tape. Trim the ends of the stems until even and place in a vase of cold water until ready to use.

Optional

Add a ribbon of your choice. Use fabric scissors to trim the ends of the ribbon at a 45-degree angle (see Ribbon on page 28).

75

WILD BLOOM

*T*his centerpiece pairs decadent dinnerplate *Dahlias* and playful *Scabiosa* pods with ghostly wisps of taupe *Cotinus*. Together they create an arrangement that is earthy and architectural. Traditionally, branches with woody stems are positioned in the vase first. They help build shape and bolster support for the more delicate stems that follow. To protect the fragile plums of *Cotinus*, this piece reverses the process, adding *Dahlias* first and the sturdy branches second. This bouquet finds its footing and sticks the landing (unlike that time I thought I was Simone Biles and tried to flip off a bar in Chattanooga) with a final addition of golden peach *Scabiosa* pods.

INGREDIENTS

| 18 STEMS | 10 STEMS | 10 STEMS |
| *DAHLIA* 'CAFÉ AU LAIT' | *COTINUS COGGYGRIA* (AKA SMOKETREE) 'YOUNG LADY' | TALL *SCABIOSA STELLATA* (AKA STARFLOWER) PODS |

COLOR PALETTE

| BLUSH | WARM TAUPE | GOLDEN PEACH | HUNTER GREEN |

TOOLS

CHICKEN WIRE
FLORAL CLIPPERS
2 PIN FROGS, LARGE
PROTECTIVE GLOVES
WATERPROOF FLORAL TAPE
WIRE CUTTERS

Flower Prep

DAHLIA

Remove all foliage and lateral blooms from the main *Dahlia* stems. Trim on a 45-degree angle and hydrate in room temperature water.

6–8"
ROOM TEMP

COTINUS

Remove any foliage from the *Cotinus* stems that may be submerged in water, retaining foliage nearest to the blooms. Crosscut the stems and hydrate in room temperature water.

6–8"
ROOM TEMP

SCABIOSA

Trim the *Scabiosa* on a 45-degree angle and hydrate in cold water.

2–4"
COLD

Vase Prep

In a large bubble bowl (approximately 7 inches tall by 10 inches wide), add large pin frogs. You may need more than 1 pin frog to cover the area of a bowl this large. Add a chicken wire pillow on top of the pin frog(s) and secure with a floral tape strap. Fill with cold water.

Shape

1. Starting low—at the opening of the vessel and continuing around its circumference—position 6 *Dahlia* stems so they drape over the lip of the vase. Our goal with this arrangement is to build height and let the blooms breathe. Gaps are okay.

2. At medium height, add 6 more *Dahlia* stems, doubling the size of the arrangement.

3. Continue to increase the height and fluff out the shape with the remaining 6 *Dahlias*. The final shape should appear more bulbous and taller than it is wide.

Pro tip

Don't forget to use your pin frogs. They are there to help secure heavy stems like *Dahlias* and *Cotinus*.

Color

4. Set aside the tallest *Cotinus* stem. With the remaining 9 *Cotinus* stems, fill in the gaps and spaces in between *Dahlias* to build volume and blend the color palette. The earthy tones of the *Cotinus* mute the saccharine pink of the *Dahlias*, bringing out their warm undertones.

5. Create asymmetry and diffuse the color by positioning the last *Cotinus* stem on the left side of the arrangement, reaching outward and up.

Depth

6. Add all 10 *Scabiosa* pods throughout the arrangement so the heads of the flowers float 1 to 2 inches beyond the other flowers. This will give the appearance of *Scabiosa* bobbing in and around the centerpiece.

79

DIFFICULTY LEVEL
advanced

SEASON
summer

MOOD
cheerful

SUMMER BREAK

*T*his bouquet of golden-hued roses and fizzy *Dahlias* recalls the long, lazy days of summers gone by. Let the nostalgic shades of hot pink transport you to a time when music was better with the windows rolled down. It didn't matter if you thought the lyrics were "We built this city on sausage rolls!" Your eyeliner was blue, your top was cropped, and your lips tasted like watermelon. You weren't just "cool." You were *funky-fresh!* So pump up the jams while you work because this playful bouquet is all about capturing the contagious joy of your youth.

INGREDIENTS

5 STEMS PEONY FOLIAGE

5 STEMS
DAHLIA 'MAGGIE C'

5 STEMS GARDEN ROSE
'CARAMEL ANTIKE'

5 STEMS MINI CALLA LILY
'PASSION FRUIT'

5 STEMS POMPON
DAHLIA 'BURLESCA'

5 TO 8
GRAPEVINE TIPS

COLOR PALETTE

COPPER · GOLDEN PEACH · SANDSTONE · PEACHY CORAL · HOT PINK · VIVID GREEN

TOOLS

BOUQUET TAPE
FLORAL CLIPPERS
PROTECTIVE GLOVES
DECORATIVE RIBBON (OPTIONAL)
FABRIC SCISSORS (OPTIONAL)

Flower Prep

PEONY FOLIAGE, GRAPEVINE

Trim the peony foliage and grapevine tips on a 45-degree angle and hydrate in warm water.

6–8"
WARM

DAHLIA

Remove all foliage from the *Dahlias*. Trim on a 45-degree angle and hydrate in cold water.

6–8"
COLD

GARDEN ROSE

Remove all foliage and thorns from the roses. Trim on a 45-degree angle and hydrate in warm water.

DEEP
WARM

MINI CALLA LILY

Remove all foliage from the mini calla lilies. Trim the ends of the stems on a 45-degree angle, leaving as much of the white tissue as possible (this helps prevent the stems from splitting), and hydrate in cold water.

2–4"
COLD

Pro tip

If the grapevine begins to wilt, recut the stems on a 45-degree angle, adding a crosscut. Place in deep hot water and into a floral cooler or refrigerator overnight (see Floral cooler on page 15). This should perk them right up.

Shape

1. Shape all 5 peony foliage stems in your hands to form a small bundle, with three distinct points reaching out and away from the center of the bouquet to the upper right, upper left, and lower left corners.

2. Starting in the center and working your way outward, widen the shape of the bouquet slightly by threading all 5 'Maggie C' *Dahlia* stems into and around the peony foliage (see Threading on page 29).

3. Increase the volume even more with all 5 garden rose stems. Float the roses so they are slightly farther out from the bouquet's center. The shape should be fluffy but not symmetrical or perfectly round.

Hey, have you played your favorite song yet? "The Sign" by Ace of Base started playing and I am living for it!

Color

4. Add a zing of hot pink by adding all 5 'Burlesca' *Dahlia* stems to the bouquet to form a triangle that travels from the bottom of the bouquet up its center and to the upper right corner.

5. Balance the color palette with the mini calla lilies. Place 4 stems evenly around the bouquet with the fifth and last stem reaching down from the lower right side.

Depth

6. Expressive and ideal for draping, vibrant grapevines bring depth and playfulness to this piece. Place 5 to 8 grapevine tips all over the bouquet. Position them to appear as if they are exploding out from all directions. Place longer stems towards the bottom of the bouquet to create a cascading effect.

7. Finish by securing the stems with bouquet tape. Trim the stems until even.

Optional

Add a ribbon of your choice. Use fabric scissors to trim the ends of the ribbon at a 45-degree angle (see Ribbon on page 28).

PERSIMMON

*W*hoever said *Chrysanthemums* are old-fashioned needs a hug. *Chrysanthemums* aren't out of fashion. They are tried and true, I'll-be-there-for-you kind of blooms, sort of like that character Janice from that '90s TV show about a group of friends living in New York. No matter how many times what's-his-face treated Janice like she was old news, there she was, waiting in the wings for someone special. Well, today is Janice's big day . . . because that someone is us!

INGREDIENTS

7 STEMS
PERSIMMON

20 STEMS
DATE PALM BERRIES

16 STEMS
CHRYSANTHEMUM
'BEVERLY BRONZE'

12 STEMS
CHRYSANTHEMUM
'SEATON'S COFFEE'

7 STEMS
ROSE 'PEACH AVALANCHE'

24 STEMS
CANARY GRASS

COLOR PALETTE

| PERSIMMON | ALLOY ORANGE | BRONZE | SMOKY GRAPEFRUIT | PALE PEACH | JADE |

TOOLS

CHICKEN WIRE
FLORAL CLIPPERS
PIN FROG, MEDIUM
PROTECTIVE GLOVES
WATERPROOF FLORAL TAPE
WIRE CUTTERS

Flower Prep

PERSIMMON, DATE PALM BERRIES, CANARY GRASS

Trim the persimmon stems, date palms, and canary grass stems on a 45-degree angle, and hydrate all the stems in room temperature water.

 4–6"
ROOM TEMP

CHRYSANTHEMUM

Remove all foliage from the *Chrysanthemum* stems. Trim on a 45-degree angle and hydrate in cold water.

 4–6"
COLD

ROSE

Remove all foliage and thorns from the rose stems. Trim on a 45-degree angle and hydrate in room temperature water.

 DEEP
ROOM TEMP

Vase Prep

In a large white tapered vase (or any large vessel—as long as it's tapered), place a chicken wire pillow on top of a large pin frog. Secure with a floral tape strap. Fill with cold water.

Shape

1. Begin with 5 stems of persimmon. Alternating between the left and right sides of the vase, add 1 stem at a time until you have created 2 low clusters: 3 stems on the left and 2 on the right. Stay low and maintain a space in between the 2 clusters. Position some of the stems so the fruit hangs over the sides.

Pro tip

Persimmons can be heavy. If imbalanced, they can tip the vase over. (Hint: Use the pin frog. It's your friend.)

2. Create asymmetry and increase the height by adding another persimmon stem rising from the center, leaning towards the right.

3. Drape the final persimmon stem over the right side to give the impression that the vase is overflowing with persimmons.

4. Create a waterfall effect by placing all 20 date palm stems into the vase (9 on the right, 11 on the left). The date palms should flow like a fountain from the center of the vase, cascading out and down the sides. Remember to use the pin frog!

Color

5. Deepen the color palette by using 13 stems of 'Beverly Bronze' *Chrysanthemum* to fill in any remaining gaps.

6. Pull the color upward by adding the remaining 3 bronze mums to the left side of the vase. Trim these stems at varying heights so the last and final stem is the tallest, creating the tip of a triangle shape.

7. Slightly above the lip of the vase, tuck 1 short 'Seaton's Coffee' *Chrysanthemum* to the left of center.

8. Add the remaining 11 *Chrysanthemums* to the right side of the arrangement. Branching out from the first stem near the center, arrange the mums so they gradually expand out and up towards the right side, creating a triangle.

Depth

9. Establish contrast by adding all 7 roses to the arrangement (don't forget to rotate your vase), breaking up the rich tones with soft points of light. A single tall stem should be placed so it reaches up and out of the right side of the piece.

10. Add 19 stems of canary grass throughout the arrangement for feathery embellishment. Position the heads of the grasses to float 1 or 2 inches beyond the arrangement.

11. Place the final 5 canary grass stems to look as if they are reaching out of the top left of the arrangement, to the sky.

DIFFICULTY LEVEL
expert

SEASON
spring

MOOD
classic

NAPOLI

This is the *one and only* occasion when we will break away from our typical design process, abandon technique, and throw caution to the wind like a toupee in a tornado. Wait! Before you feel betrayed and throw the book across the room, let me explain. Inspired by the European aesthetic of floral design, this piece is a glorious mass of flowers stuffed with tulips, crammed with roses, and fit to burst with *Freesia*. In order to achieve an arrangement of this density, we will need to . . . well . . . build out . . . *everything at the same time.* Yes. Shape, color, and depth. Think of it like decorating a layered cake, stacking layers upon layers until we have one big, beautiful, bodacious work of art. You got it? Good!

INGREDIENTS

20 STEMS
SPRAY ROSE 'AURELIA'

18 STEMS
PARROT TULIP 'APRICOT'

15 STEMS
ANTHRISCUS SYLVESTRIS
'RAVENSWING'

10 STEMS
FREESIA, GOLD

COLOR PALETTE

| CLEMENTINE | ARANCIA | COFFEE | BERGAMOT |

Flower Prep

SPRAY ROSE

Remove all foliage and thorns from the spray roses. Do not remove lateral blooms until you get to step 1. Trim on a 45-degree angle and hydrate in warm water.

 DEEP
WARM

PARROT TULIP

Even as a cut flower, tulips continue to grow, causing the petals and stems to become pliable. Remove all foliage. Keeping the stems tall, trim on a 45-degree angle and hydrate in cool water. Store in a cool area, floral cooler, or refrigerator until ready to use (see Floral cooler on page 15).

 4–6"
COOL

FREESIA, ANTHRISCUS

Remove all lateral blooms from the *Freesia* stems. Trim *Freesia* and *Anthriscus* stems on a 45-degree angle and hydrate in cold water.

 2–4"
COLD

Vase Prep

In a tapered vase (a wooden one, if you have it!), place a chicken wire pillow. Secure with a floral tape strap. Fill with cold water.

Shape/Color/Depth

1. Pull 7 spray rose stems from the bunch. Snip any lateral blooms that have a stem length longer than 2 inches from the main stems. This should yield about 20 additional itty-bitty stems, plus the original 7 stems.

2. Build the first layer with the 27 spray rose stems from step 1 and 5 parrot tulip stems. This layer should resemble a stout dome or muffin top. Position the bulk of the stems to face out around the lip of the vase. The remaining flowers in the middle should loosely obscure the chicken wire.

3. Add 6 medium-length spray roses, 3 parrot tulips, and 5 *Anthriscus* stems to build out a second layer. This layer should be wider than it is tall. Direct the bulk of the flowers to the left and right sides of the vase with a small portion going to the middle for balance. Use the *Anthriscus* to create the illusion that the flowers are tumbling out of the vase.

4. With the remaining 7 spray rose stems, 5 parrot tulips, and the remaining 10 *Anthriscus*, create a third layer that looks like two large mounds dramatically rising from the depths of the vase. (Now go back and read that last bit like you are a drama teacher trying to impress your students. Fun, right?!) There should be a clear dip in the middle of this layer.

5. Place 10 *Freesia* stems throughout the arrangement. The *Freesia* should float 1 or 2 inches away from the main body of the arrangement.

6. Create the final layer by placing the remaining 5 parrot tulips in positions of prominence. Be sure to keep the space in the middle free from any flowers that could diminish its impact.

Yay! Look at that bulbous beauty. This is a hefty honey of an arrangement, and I am so proud of you for diving into this work and sticking with it.

This arrangement illustrates that there is more than one way to create. It is a reminder that it's okay to challenge the status quo in your world. Through the thoughtful exploration of alternative ideas and paths, you can build a lifestyle that supports the magic that makes you you.

MOLASSES

*T*his harvest of 'Arguta' spirea elevates any arrangement with its pencil-thin branches and dramatic architectural shape. Notice how this cultivar is just beginning to sprout with life as baby buds of green start to unfurl. Delight in the dramatic composition of the *Ranunculus* as warping shades of chocolate orange orbit rich tones of molasses. Grab a hot drink and find comfort in knowing that it is unlikely that the hellebores will wilt. They have matured over the winter months in anticipation of an early spring harvest and are ready to be crafted into a ravishing spray of splendor.

INGREDIENTS

| 15 STEMS
SPIREA 'ARGUTA' | 16 STEMS HELLEBORE
'IVORY PRINCE' | 30 STEMS *RANUNCULUS*
'CAFÉ AU LAIT' |

COLOR PALETTE

| WASABI | HONEYDEW | MOLASSES | CHOCOLATE ORANGE |

CHICKEN WIRE
FLORAL CLIPPERS
PIN FROG, LARGE
PROTECTIVE GLOVES
WATERPROOF FLORAL TAPE
WIRE CUTTERS

Flower Prep

SPIREA

Crosscut the spirea and hydrate in warm water. If the spirea have already started to flower, store them in a cool area, floral cooler, or refrigerator (see Floral cooler on page 15).

 DEEP
WARM

HELLEBORE

Remove any foliage from the hellebore stems that may sit in water. Submerge the ends of the stems in water to trim on a 45-degree angle and immediately hydrate in cold water.

 3–5"
COLD

RANUNCULUS

Remove all foliage from the *Ranunculus* stems. Trim on a 45-degree angle and hydrate.

 4–6"
COLD

Vase Prep

I used a shallow concrete bowl with a wide mouth, but any similar bowl will work as long as it is low and tapered. Place a chicken wire pillow on top of a pin frog. Secure with a floral tape strap. Fill with cold water.

Shape

1. Set aside 3 long, expressive spirea stems.

2. Cut up and divide the remaining 12 spirea into shorter pieces (each approximately 8 to 10 inches long), effectively doubling the quantity. Divide the stems into two groups of approximately 12 stems each.

3. On the right side of the vase, position one group of spirea so the stems reach away from the center of the vase—some reaching towards the front and back sides, with the majority of the spirea stretching out from the right side of the vase. Repeat this process with the second group of stems on the left side of the vase to create two distinct shapes with a visible gap in the middle.

4. Starting left of center and working outward, add the 3 expressive stems of spirea you set aside in step 1 to create drama and asymmetry.

Color

5. Place 1 short hellebore stem in the middle of the arrangement. Cluster 6 more hellebores on the right side of the vase and the remaining 9 hellebores on the opposite side. This should create 2 distinct hellebore clouds nestled in and around the spirea.

Depth

6. Set aside the 5 tallest stems of *Ranunculus*. Using 12 of the remaining stems, stay low to fill in the spaces around the hellebore.

7. With the last 13 stems, work from the center of the arrangement outward to build height, creating a loose cloud of medium height.

8. Finally, place the 5 reserved *Ranunculus* stems in the arrangement so they appear to be stretching out and up towards the sky.

Pro tip

Select hellebore stems that have developed a bulbous seedpod. This indicates that the stems were harvested from a plant whose flowers had successfully matured throughout the growing season. Mature hellebore will have a longer vase life.

95

Yellow

DIFFICULTY LEVEL
beginner

SEASON
autumn

MOOD
bold

GOLDENROD

A handful of golden rain tree pods can easily take any arrangement from basic to BAM! faster than you can say "Parker Posey picked a perfect peony!" Not only are they the star of this arrangement, but they love to share the spotlight, graciously elevating even the most common of blooms to their level. Pairing these golden-warm hues with shades of buttercup and amber tells a color story of mulled cider as it wafts through the house on a crisp autumn night. Time to cue up *The Goonies* and fill your mugs because this fella is the perfect autumnal companion.

INGREDIENTS

20 STEMS *KOELREUTERIA PANICULATA* (AKA GOLDEN RAIN TREE) PODS

5 STEMS *BANKSIA BAXTERI* (AKA BIRD'S NEST BANKSIA)

5 STEMS SUNFLOWER 'RUBY ECLIPSE'

12 STEMS *RUDBECKIA* 'SAHARA'

COLOR PALETTE

GOLD   LIME   BUTTERCUP   SAHARA

TOOLS

PROTECTIVE GLOVES
FLORAL CLIPPERS
CHICKEN WIRE
WIRE CUTTERS
WATERPROOF FLORAL TAPE

Flower Prep

BANKSAIA, RAIN TREE PODS

Remove all foliage from the rain tree pod stems. Trim the *Banksia* and golden rain tree pods on a 45-degree angle and hydrate in cold water.

 6–8"
COLD

SUNFLOWER, RUDBECKIA

Trim the sunflower and *Rudbeckia* stems on a 45-degree angle and hydrate in cold water. Store the *Rudbeckia* in a cool area, floral cooler, or refrigerator until ready to use (see Floral cooler on page 15).

 4–6"
COLD

Pro tip

When sourcing *Rudbeckia*, select blooms that have not fully opened. Beware of speckles and dark spots. Discoloration is a sign that the flowers are beginning to stale.

Vase Prep

If you do not have a large stone vase like the one pictured, any opaque cylindrical vase will work. Add a chicken wire pillow and secure with a floral tape strap. Fill with cold water.

Shape

1. Set aside half of the golden rain tree pods. Divide the remaining 10 stems into three smaller bunches (two bunches of 3 stems each and one bunch of 4 stems). Trim the stems in each bunch so they range in length: One bunch should have 6-inch-long stems, one should have 10-inch-long stems, and the final bunch should have 12-inch-long stems.

2. Leaving some clear spaces for the *Banksia*, place the shortest bunch of stems into the chicken wire pillow, creating a small mound.

3. Add the medium-length stems to the arrangement so they drape over the sides, reaching out to create an oblong shape that is wider than it is tall.

4. Exaggerate the shape by adding the longest stems to the arrangement.

5. Using the 10 golden rain tree pods set aside in step 1, build out the shape. It should feel tall, wide, and airy.

Color

6. Add all 5 *Banksia* stems, cropped close to the lip of the vase and filling the gaps left by the golden rain tree pods. Place at least 2 blooms front and center to allow the bright lime to pop out from the arrangement rather than getting buried.

Depth

7. Add all 5 sunflowers of medium height to the arrangement. Focus their placement towards the center.

8. Staying within the outermost edges created by the golden rain tree pods, create depth by placing 10 'Sahara' *Rudbeckia* stems. The *Rudbeckia*, extending in all directions, should float in front of the *Banksia* and sunflowers.

9. Place 1 tall *Rudbeckia* so it reaches out from the bottom left side of the arrangement. Rotate your vessel and place the final *Rudbeckia* on the bottom left side of the back of your arrangement. Imagine these 2 stems have discovered a patch of sunshine the other flowers have not, and they are determined to stretch themselves towards it.

You've done it. You have crafted a stunning centerpiece of amber bathed in golden light! Take a moment to appreciate your work. Remember, you deserve this.

MIMOSA

Success is defined by balance. The ability to balance your goals, root yourself in the present, and appreciate what you already have—that is true success.

DIFFICULTY LEVEL
beginner

SEASON
winter

MOOD
drama queen

MIMOSA

*I*t's the moment of dread. It is the gut punch when you realize that in your haste to prepare your home for hosting brunch you forgot the most important thing: *flowers*. As reality closes in, the walls begin to warp and your velvet jumpsuit feels six sizes too small. With only twenty minutes until a swarm of busybodies clamor upon your doorstep, you question if it was a wise choice to have spent that extra hour hand calligraphing name cards. In an instant, you snap out of your reverie and remember who and what you are: an incredible creative master. A swift fashioning of flowers into a stunning centerpiece is elementary compared to the big magic you can muster. With its bold form and mellow color palette, this arrangement comes together to tell a color story of effortless grandeur, impressing even the most critical of guests.

INGREDIENTS

5 STEMS
ASHBY'S BANKSIA

12 STEMS
GARDEN ROSE
'YELLOW POMPON'

COLOR PALETTE

KIWI

MARMALADE

TUSCANY

Flower Prep

BANKSIA

Remove three-quarters of the lower
foliage on the *Banksia*, including
any foliage that will be in water.
Crosscut the stems and hydrate
in room temperature water.

8–10"
ROOM TEMP

GARDEN ROSE

Remove all foliage and thorns
from the roses. Trim on a
45-degree angle and hydrate
in room temperature water.

DEEP
ROOM TEMP

Vase Prep

If a vase with a rustic, weathered
veneer is not available, any tall
vase with a narrow mouth will
work. Add cold water to your
vessel until 90 percent full.

Shape

1. Place all 5 Ashby's Banksia stems in the left side of the vase.
   Orient the stems so the heads point in different directions.
   Gradually increase the height of the arrangement with each
   additional stem, adding volume to the shape.

Color

2. Cluster 8 garden roses to form a soft cloud positioned low,
   near the opening of the vase. The blooms closest to the mouth
   of the vase should hang over the edge and cover the lip.

3. Add 2 longer rose stems to stretch the color upward and
   down to the left side of the vase.

*At this point it is safe to say your brilliant mind
has mastered this design. If you are feeling
extra, feel free to add a little of your own style
to this arrangement. Your personality is what we
love most about you. Put some of that magic
into these flowers.*

Depth

4. Dramatically increase the height with the last 2 tall rose
   stems. Place them so they dramatically flare out to the right
   side. These stems may not be long enough to reach the
   bottom of the vase—that is okay. As long as the bottoms
   are submerged in 2 to 3 inches of water, they will remain
   hydrated.

Look at that! You made that arrangement and there is still time left to make yourself a cocktail before the guests arrive. Well done!

DIFFICULTY LEVEL
advanced

SEASON
summer

MOOD
classic

LEMON CHIFFON

A spoonful of creamy marigolds, succulent passion fruit, and iridescent *Celosia* frolic through this arrangement to tickle our somber sensibilities to life. Practically perfect in every way, this piece is a perfect gift for yourself. Oh yes, that's right. Perhaps you thought I was going to tell you to give this arrangement to someone else? NOPE. As your unofficial best flower friend, it is my duty to remind you to keep for yourself what is often given to others. Sometimes it is okay to say "MINE." This is one of those times.

INGREDIENTS

13 STEMS *PASSIFLORA INCARNATA* (AKA FRUITING PASSION VINE)

16 STEMS MARIGOLD 'WHITE SWAN'

10 STEMS CHINA ASTER 'TOWER YELLOW'

8 STEMS *CELOSIA* 'SUPERCREST'

COLOR PALETTE

CHAMOIS   SWEET CREAM   LEMON CHIFFON   GOLDEN CORAL

CHICKEN WIRE
FLORAL CLIPPERS
PROTECTIVE GLOVES
WATERPROOF FLORAL TAPE
WIRE CUTTERS
LARGE WATERPROOF LINER (OPTIONAL)

Flower Prep

PASSIFLORA

Remove all foliage from the fruiting passion vine. Trim on a 45-degree angle and hydrate in cool water in a narrow vase, which prevents the thin stems from falling out of the water under the weight of the hulking fruit.

4–6"
COOL

MARIGOLD, CHINA ASTER, CELOSIA

Remove all foliage from the marigold, China aster, and *Celosia* stems. Trim on a 45-degree angle and hydrate in cold water.

6–8"
COLD

Vase Prep

In a cylindrical vase of medium height, add a chicken wire pillow and secure with a floral tape strap. If the vase is not waterproof, add a liner (see Waterproofing on page 30). Here's hoping you don't learn the hard way like I did. Yeesh.

Shape

1. Carefully drape all 13 fruiting passion vines around the left and right sides of the vase. Leave a clear space in the center. Trim the stems at different lengths so they fall over the edge of the vase in layers.

Color

2. Fill in the gaps using all 16 marigold stems. Use a mix of stem heights. Position the stems to form a wiry, unkempt dome with broad spaces between each stem.

3. Balance the shape with 7 stems of China aster, filling in the gaps and spaces left behind by the jutting marigold. The arrangement should begin to feel lush, pastel, and delicate.

Depth

4. Convey depth with 6 *Celosia* stems, precisely trimmed to nuzzle into the crevices around the marigold and aster.

5. Add the 2 tallest *Celosia* stems to the left side of the arrangement to craft asymmetry and encourage the eye to travel up.

6. Lastly, increase the height of the arrangement by placing the remaining 3 asters on the left side of the arrangement. Position the stems at differing heights to amplify asymmetry.

So how did you do? Are you happy with your creation? Are you disappointed or feeling a bit "meh" about it? It is important to remember that no matter the outcome, you have taken the time to care for yourself in a profoundly creative way. That is a beautiful thing. Keep coming back. It gets better.

Pro tip

If an arrangement feels too
angular, adding a stem or two that
curves towards the center of an
arrangement adds whimsy
and can soften the sharp lines of
an asymmetric form.

DIFFICULTY LEVEL
beginner

SEASON
spring

MOOD
whimsical

CANARY

*T*he emergence of bulb flowers during the first flush of spring can only mean one thing ... party time! No different from an elusive friend sauntering into the party two hours late brandishing a leaked copy of the latest Rihanna album, these midseason beauties know how to make an entrance. This canary-hued bouquet sings of the romance of spring, where chests swell at the sight of blossoming *Freesia* and the air is electrified with the sound of happy pollinators buzzing about.

INGREDIENTS

6 STEMS
FREESIA, WHITE

12 STEMS *RANUNCULUS*
'TECOLOTE GOLD'

6 STEMS BUTTERFLY
DAFFODIL 'ORANGERY'

20 STEMS *FRITILLARIA
UVA-VULPIS* (AKA FOX'S
GRAPE FRITILLARY)

COLOR PALETTE

IVORY   CANARY   YUZU   SULFUR

BOUQUET TAPE
FLORAL CLIPPERS
PROTECTIVE GLOVES
DECORATIVE RIBBON (OPTIONAL)
FABRIC SCISSORS (OPTIONAL)

Flower Prep

FREESIA

Remove all lateral blooms
from the main *Freesia* stems.
Trim on a 45-degree angle
and hydrate in cold water.

4–6"
COLD

RANUNCULUS

Remove all foliage from the
Ranunculus stems. Trim
on a 45-degree angle and
hydrate in cold water.

4–6"
COLD

BUTTERFLY DAFFODIL

Remove all foliage from the daffodil
stems. Trim on a 45-degree angle
and, since daffodils tend to leak, set
aside to drain and hydrate in cold
water (see Leaking stems on page 25).

2–4"
COLD

FRITILLARIA

Trim the fritillary stems on a
45-degree angle, but do not remove
the foliage. Hydrate in cold water.

4–6"
COLD

Shape

1. Gather 6 stems of *Freesia* into your hands to form an
   asymmetrical cloud, with the upper right corner reaching
   higher than the left.

Color

2. Add 10 *Ranunculus* stems to the arrangement. Start in the
   upper left corner and work on a downward diagonal towards
   the lower right corner.

3. Add the last 2 *Ranunculus* stems to the far-right side of the
   arrangement to draw the color through the body of the
   bouquet.

4. Cluster all 6 butterfly daffodil stems on the right side of the
   arrangement to fill out the shape, intensifying the color as it
   fans out and down the right side of the bouquet.

*Heads up! The depth steps require delicacy
as the dainty fritillary stems are added to the
bouquet. Be patient with the process and most of
all . . . yourself.*

Depth

5. Gently thread 1 fritillary stem into the center of the bouquet
   (see Threading on page 29). Add 2 more stems to the center
   section of the arrangement a few inches apart.

6. Position 9 fritillary stems to create a curved spray of green
   and sulfur erupting from the right side of the bouquet.

7. Tuck the remaining 8 fritillary stems along the entire border.
   Position the heads of the blooms to loosely frame the blaze of
   yellow and white flowers.

8. Finish by securing the stems with bouquet tape. Trim the
   stems until even. Hydrate in a vase of cold water until ready
   to use.

Optional

Add a ribbon of your choice. Use fabric
scissors to trim the ends of the ribbon at a
45-degree angle (see Ribbon on page 28).

POMELO AND LAVENDER

*T*riumphant and beautiful, this fresh take on the pastel fancies of spring is a giant confection of creamy pomelo and sumptuous lavender. The buttery yellow tulips dazzle, exploding into a double layer of silken petals. With their golden sepals and trumpets of sugared lavender, the tall campaniles of *Paulownia* are nothing short of miraculous. Add a handful of exploding tulips and the beauty of this piece is more than memorable; it's legendary.

INGREDIENTS

12 STEMS	7 STEMS	10 STEMS	12 STEMS
PAULOWNIA TOMENTOSA	*ALSTROEMERIA* 'RIO'	GARDEN ROSE 'CATALINA'	DARWIN DOUBLE TULIP 'AKEBONO'

COLOR PALETTE

LAVENDER	BANANA	POMELO	CLOVER LIME

TOOLS

CHICKEN WIRE
FLORAL CLIPPERS
PROTECTIVE GLOVES
WATERPROOF FLORAL TAPE
WIRE CUTTERS
LARGE WATERPROOF LINER (OPTIONAL)
BOUQUET TAPE
FLORAL WIRE

Flower Prep

PAULOWNIA

Crosscut the *Paulownia* stems and hydrate in warm water. Store at room temperature. Keep out of direct sunlight. Handle with care as the blooms can easily bruise.

 5–7"
WARM

ALSTROEMERIA, DARWIN DOUBLE TULIP

Remove all foliage from the *Alstroemeria*. Trim the *Alstroemeria* and tulip stems, keeping the tulips tall, on a 45-degree angle and hydrate in cold water.

 4–6"
COLD

GARDEN ROSE

Remove all foliage and thorns from the roses. Trim on a 45-degree angle and hydrate in room temperature water.

 DEEP
ROOM TEMP

Vase Prep

In an extra-large bowl, secure a pillow of chicken wire with a floral tape strap. If the bowl is not waterproofed, you will need to add a liner (see Waterproofing on page 30).

Shape

1. Divide 5 stems of *Paulownia* into 10 shorter stems. Add these 10 stems to the vase, working low and leaving gaps between stems. This shape will serve as the foundation for the larger, heavier stems to follow.

2. Leaving the center open, stay to the left and right sides of the vase and add the remaining 7 *Paulownia*. Using the stems' differing heights to your advantage, create two large sloping clusters of the lavender-hued *Paulownia* flowers.

Color

3. Place 2 stems of *Alstroemeria* low, in the center of the vase. Distribute the remaining 5 stems evenly throughout, using the deepest yellow *Alstroemeria* to fill in the gaps and mask the mechanics.

4. Working your way from low to high, add all 10 garden roses to the arrangement. Maintain the depression in the middle of the arrangement. Do not tuck the roses in—position them so their ruffled heads float.

Depth

5. Set aside the tallest and juiciest Darwin double tulip stem for step 6. Around the circumference of the vase, drape 5 tulips just over the lip of the vessel. Avoiding the center, use 6 tulips of medium or tall height to soften and round out the shape of the clusters.

6. To the right of center, place the juicy, dramatic tallest tulip. Use the hardier stems surrounding the tulip as support.

Pro tip

If necessary, use a mossy green-colored bouquet tape and a length of floral wire to fortify the stems of tulips.

119

DIFFICULTY LEVEL
beginner

SEASON
summer

MOOD
energetic

BUMBLEBEE

*I*f an unexpected detour happens to lead you through a field of blooming wildflowers, don't question it! The wisest of us welcome the chance to pluck fresh flowers until our arms are loaded with a harvest of happiness. If you paused gathering from the abundant beds of poppy and primrose to quietly observe a bee rhythmically dart from flower to flower to flower, that would be sensible. If that vision inspired you to make a bouquet buzzing with buds of golden *Rudbeckia*, cloud white *Dahlias*, and ruffled marigolds, well my dear, that would be a fantasy!

INGREDIENTS

5 STEMS *DAHLIA* 'SEATTLE'

6 STEMS POMPON *DAHLIA* 'WHITE ASTER'

5 STEMS AZTEC MARIGOLD

13 STEMS RUDBECKIA 'YELLOW CONEFLOWER'

COLOR PALETTE

MIMOSA CLOUD WHITE MARIGOLD BUMBLEBEE

Flower Prep

DAHLIA

Remove all foliage from the *Dahlia* stems. Trim on a 45-degree angle and hydrate in cold water. Store the *Dahlias* in a cool area, floral cooler, or refrigerator until ready to use (see Floral cooler on page 15).

6–8"
COLD

MARIGOLD

Remove all foliage from the marigold stems. Trim on a 45-degree angle and hydrate in cold water.

6–8"
COLD

RUDBECKIA

Preserve any lateral blooms towards the top of the *Rudbeckia* stems. Remove any foliage and lateral blooms below 5 inches from the primary bloom. Trim on a 45-degree angle and hydrate in cold water.

6–8"
COLD

Shape

1. Gather 5 'Seattle' *Dahlia* stems to form a soft, round shape. This is the core of the bouquet and will help support the more expressive blooms in the forthcoming steps.

2. Working on a downward diagonal from the upper right corner to the lower left corner, divide 6 stems of 'White Aster' pompon *Dahlias* into two groups and place 3 stems on either side of the bouquet. (Oh my gosh, did I just do math without a calculator?! This calls for Champagne! BRB!)

Color

3. Set aside the juiciest, fullest marigold stem for step 5. Create a triangle with the remaining 4 marigold stems. Place the marigolds so they travel down the center of the arrangement and into the lower right corner of the bouquet. Allow these blooms to float 1 to 2 inches away from the *Dahlias* so the marigold color is in the foreground.

Depth

4. Add all 13 *Rudbeckia* stems to the bouquet. Place the majority of the stems around the border and a few dispersed throughout the body of the bouquet. Create depth by gently pulling some stems out by 2 to 3 inches so they float in front of the other flowers.

5. Bring balance to the bouquet and exaggerate the shape with the marigold stem you set aside in step 3. Place it in the upper right corner of the bouquet.

6. Finish by securing the stems with bouquet tape. Trim the stems until even. Hydrate in a vase of cold water until ready to use.

Optional

Add a ribbon of your choice. Use fabric scissors to trim the ends of the ribbon at a 45-degree angle (see Ribbon on page 28).

Pro tip

When sourcing *Rudbeckia*, select
blooms that have not fully opened.
Beware of speckles and dark spots.
Discoloration is a sign that the
flowers are beginning to stale.

DIFFICULTY LEVEL
beginner

SEASON
summer

MOOD
cheerful

LEMONADE

With petite blossoms of bright yellow *Lysimachia* exploding off their darkly trimmed branches like firecrackers in the night, this arrangement is a burst of light sent from the flower gods. *Lysimachia*—with its abundant, flourishing branches—quickly fill out the shape and make our work simple. *Lysimachia* are magic; they are the soul of this arrangement. The addition of softly colored 'Xanthos' cosmos florets creates an angelic glow that offsets the dark bole-hued leaves of the *Lysimachia*. Though it may look complicated, I assure you this blonde bombshell of an arrangement is as easy to make as a pitcher of lemonade.

INGREDIENTS

20 STEMS FLOWERING
LYSIMACHIA CILIATA
'FIRECRACKER'

10 STEMS *DAHLIA*
'YELLOW HEAVEN'

10 STEMS SWEET PEA
'JILLY'

25 STEMS *COSMOS*
'XANTHOS'

COLOR PALETTE

BOLE BRIGHT YELLOW LEMONADE CREAM BUTTERMILK

TOOLS

CHICKEN WIRE
FLORAL CLIPPERS
PROTECTIVE GLOVES
WATERPROOF FLORAL TAPE
WIRE CUTTERS
LARGE WATERPROOF LINER (OPTIONAL)

Flower Prep

LYSIMACHIA, SWEET PEA

Trim the ends of the *Lysimachia* and sweet pea stems on a 45-degree angle and hydrate in room temperature water.

4–6"
ROOM TEMP

DAHLIA

Remove all foliage and lateral blooms from the main *Dahlia* stems. Trim on a 45-degree angle and hydrate in cold water. Store in a cool area, floral cooler, or refrigerator until ready to use (see Floral cooler on page 15).

6–8"
COLD

COSMOS

Preserve any lateral blooms towards the top of the *Cosmos* stem. Remove any foliage and lateral blooms below 5 inches from the primary bloom. Trim on a 45-degree angle and hydrate in cold water.

6–8"
COLD

Vase Prep

In a waterproof metal bucket of medium height, add a floral tape grid. Secure the grid with a floral tape ring. For this piece, I cleaned an old bucket I found in my garage and waterproofed it with a liner (see Waterproofing on page 30).

Shape

1. Use 14 *Lysimachia* stems to create a wild and expressive domed shape, with its many laterals reaching out to the sides.

2. Maintaining a clear space in the center, add 5 tall *Lysimachia* stems to the left side of the arrangement. The added stems should appear to jut out of the upper left side.

3. Add the final *Lysimachia* stem to shoot up and out from the right side of the arrangement.

Color

4. Set aside 3 of the tallest *Dahlias* for step 6.

5. Before adding the remaining 7 stems to the arrangement, trim a few (4 or 5) so they can be placed very low, positioned as if they are cautiously rising from the base of the arrangement. Trim the other 2 or 3 so they sit slightly higher when placed.

Hey, let's check in. How are you feeling? Remember that perfection is not the goal. The goal is for you to take time away from a hectic schedule to give yourself space to be creative. To honor yourself with an opportunity to commune with nature. To remind yourself that you are worthy of beauty. That is what this time is for.

6. Add the final 3 *Dahlias* to the arrangement. Avoid the space in the center of the arrangement. Stacking the *Dahlias* just to the left and right of center supports a clear color story.

Depth

7. Stay low to add all 10 sweet pea stems around the left and right sides of the arrangement. Leave space in the middle.

8. Working outward from the middle of the arrangement, begin adding the *Cosmos*. Start low and in the center with a few (3 to 5) shorter stems and work outward.

9. Allow the *Cosmos* to gradually increase in height as you work from the center out, until the tallest stems are stretching up and out from both sides of the arrangement. Apportion the *Cosmos* evenly throughout the arrangement.

127

Green

DIFFICULTY LEVEL
beginner

SEASON
summer

MOOD
whimsical

DAY GLOW

*A*s though plucked from the weathered trellis of a forgotten Biergarten, these hops, with their scaly bracts and petite conical form, are elegantly twisted and twined together to fashion a roughly hewn hoop of lupulin-rich delights. Hops dry beautifully and—if left undisturbed—can last for months as a dried display. Sensible, right? Displaying a world of colors from matcha to limerita, this frameless wreath is decidedly dimensional in its simplicity.

INGREDIENTS

9 STEMS HOPS ON THE VINE 'CASCADE' (3 TO 5 FEET IN LENGTH EACH)

COLOR PALETTE

MATCHA	DAY GLOW	LIMERITA

BIND WIRE
FLORAL CLIPPERS
PROTECTIVE GLOVES
WIRE CLIPPERS
DECORATIVE RIBBON
FABRIC SCISSORS

Flower Prep

HOP VINES

Trim the ends of the hop vines
and hydrate in cold water.

 4–6"
COLD

Shape/Color/Depth

1. Lightly twirl all 9 hop vines around one another to form a loose twist.

2. Pull the ends together to form a circle and tuck the less desirable stems behind or underneath the more visually pleasing vine tips.

3. Use bind wire to secure the ends of the vines together.

4. From end to end, lightly wrap the entire wreath in bind wire. This will create a bit of structure.

5. Tie a knot and clip the ends of the wire using the wire clippers. If there are a few trailing pieces or wayward vines that look askew, that's okay. The unruly nature of this design is what makes it appear effortless. Besides, you and I both know the only thing we need to be worried about "reining in" is our obsession with malted waffles.

6. Using a slipknot (or any kind of knot, for that matter), add a ribbon of your choice. Use fabric scissors to trim the ends of the ribbon at a 45-degree angle (see Ribbon on page 28).

133

ARCTIC LIME

*J*ust squish it! Well, okay, maybe "squish" is an inarticulate way of saying "snuggle." If we squished the flowers in the literal sense, they would be a hideous lump of green mush. In the words of the great Valerie Cherish, "I don't want to see that!" So I take it back. No squishing! This design offers an opportunity to create a color story that has been stitched together like a beautiful patchwork quilt. Requiring minimal blending, this quickly assembled bouquet is the closest us creative junkies might ever get to feeling instant gratification.

INGREDIENTS

8 STEMS FRESH *QUERCUS RUBRA* (AKA RED OAK) FOLIAGE

2 STEMS *HYDRANGEA* 'LIMELIGHT'

5 STEMS *DAHLIA* 'POLKA'

7 STEMS LISIANTHUS 'ROSITA GREEN'

3 STEMS *ZINNIA* 'QUEEN LIME'

COLOR PALETTE

VIVID GREEN   CHETWODE   RHUBARB   VANILLA   ARCTIC LIME   CHARTREUSE

BOUQUET TAPE
FLORAL CLIPPERS
PROTECTIVE GLOVES
DECORATIVE RIBBON (OPTIONAL)
FABRIC SCISSORS (OPTIONAL)

Flower Prep

OAK FOLIAGE, HYDRANGEA

Crosscut the oak foliage
and *Hydrangea* stems and
hydrate in warm water.

 DEEP
WARM

DAHLIA

Remove all foliage and any lateral
blooms from the *Dahlia* stems.
Submerge the stems in water
to trim on a 45-degree angle.
Immediately hydrate in cold
water and store in a cool place,
floral cooler, or a refrigerator
(see Floral cooler on page 15).

 DEEP
COLD

LISIANTHUS, ZINNIA

Remove all foliage from the lisianthus
and *Zinnia* stems. Separate and put
aside any lateral blooms growing
off the primary stems. Trim on a
45-degree angle and hydrate in cold
water. Store in a cool place, floral
cooler, or refrigerator until ready to
use (see Floral cooler on page 15).

 6–8"
COLD

Shape

1. Lay the foundation for the bouquet by gathering all 8 oak foliage stems in your hands to make a loose cloud.

2. Add the 2 *Hydrangea* stems to the upper right corner to build out an asymmetric shape.

Color

3. Add all 5 *Dahlia* stems to the left of the *Hydrangea* to resemble the letter *J*. The vanilla and rhubarb colors should hug (not squish!) the *Hydrangea* as they travel down and to the bottom left corner of the bouquet.

Depth

4. In the seat of the colorful *J*, stack all 7 stems of lisianthus with one on top of the other until the last and tallest stem is slightly higher than the neighboring *Dahlia*.

5. Create depth by pulling some of the lisianthus stems forward to float slightly farther out than the others.

6. In the central section of the bouquet, place all 3 *Zinnia* stems at different heights to create a triangle. Position the *Zinnias* at different depths to allow some of the blooms to float an inch away from the body. Play with depth to find a combination you prefer.

7. Finish by securing the stems with bouquet tape. Trim the stems until even and place in a vase of cold water until ready to use.

Optional

Add a ribbon of your choice. Use fabric
scissors to trim the ends of the ribbon at a
45-degree angle (see Ribbon on page 28).

If you're feeling a little sad that your time creating this bouquet is over, I've got your back, boo. Turn this design session into a fabulous photo shoot. When you're done, post your creation to social media with the caption: Decided to trade piles of dirty laundry for piles of beautiful flowers. "Why?" you ask? The question you should be asking is "Why not?" #winning #flowersareselfcare

DIFFICULTY LEVEL
advanced

SEASON
summer

MOOD
bold

ARTICHOKE

*N*o instructional text about floral design is complete without an edible arrangement. Well … mostly edible. I would avoid eating the stems and leaves of the pear branches. And the red-flower currant is as bitter as a jilted lover. But the mint, crab apples, and artichokes are edible! Wait. No, at this stage they are not ripe and probably taste terrible as well. I guess the lesson here is even though an arrangement is beautiful and allegedly edible, it can still taste like a shoe. Still, that's no reason to avoid using the mint. Mojitos for everybody!

INGREDIENTS

2 STEMS
EUROPEAN PEAR TREE
FOLIAGE

9 STEMS
RIBES SANGUINEUM
(AKA RED-FLOWER
CURRANT) FOLIAGE
'KING EDWARD VII'

11 STEMS
CRAB APPLE TIPS

5 STEMS
'CHOCOLATE MINT'

5 STEMS
GLOBE ARTICHOKE
'IMPERIAL STAR'

COLOR PALETTE

BRIGHT GREEN   MIDWAY GREEN   BARN RED   MINT   ARTICHOKE

CHICKEN WIRE
FLORAL CLIPPERS
PIN FROG, SMALL
PROTECTIVE GLOVES
WATERPROOF FLORAL TAPE
WIRE CLIPPERS

Flower Prep

Remove any foliage that may be in the water in the final arrangement from the pear stems, *Ribes*, crab apple tips, mint, and artichokes. Trim stems on a 45-degree angle and hydrate in cold water.

 4–6"
COLD

Vase Prep

Place the pin frog in a small urn (the vase seen here is about 6 inches tall). Add a chicken wire pillow on top of the pin frog and secure with a floral tape strap.

Shape

1. Place both stems of pear tree foliage low on the left and right sides of the vase.

2. Use 8 low to medium-long stems of *Ribes* to fill in any gaps and build a shape that resembles a small hill.

3. Create an asymmetric shape with the final, tall *Ribes* stem by placing it left of center.

Color

4. Staying fairly low, fill in the remaining gaps with 6 crabapple stems. Add 4 additional stems to drape out of the side of the vase to give the appearance that the arrangement is bursting to life with fruiting branches.

5. Add the final, tall crabapple stem to the right side of the arrangement.

Depth

6. Enrich the color palette by clustering all 5 'Chocolate Mint' stems of medium length to the outer left side of the arrangement.

Hi, flower friend. We are about to add the artichokes. These can be tricky to add into an arrangement that already has plenty of stems in it. If you begin to feel frustrated, take a moment to notice where that feeling sits in your body. Then try taking a few deep breaths. Remember to give yourself a bit of grace. Be patient with the process and yourself.

7. Evenly disperse all 5 artichoke stems throughout the arrangement. Allow the artichokes to be the focal point by positioning their stems to face out and float in front of the other blooms.

Bon appétit! No, not really. Tastes like a shoe,
remember? Sure is purdy, though!

GREENWOOD

As long as there are flowers, there
are reminders everywhere that beauty
exists. Where there is beauty, there is hope.
It is all around us. We just have to
train our eyes to see it.

DIFFICULTY LEVEL
beginner

SEASON
autumn

MOOD
whimsical

GREENWOOD

*T*his arrangement is more than a centerpiece, it is a sprawling tablescape of earthborn textures. The layers of richly hued pumpkins change this spooky palette into a fairy-tale composition of mythical beauty. Thoughtfully arranged on a bed of moss, the only thing missing from this magical harvest of gourds is a mischievous woodland creature for a sidekick. Oh, and a hunky elf. This color story is definitely missing a hunky elf.

INGREDIENTS

4 TO 6 FEET OF
PRESERVED
MOSS SHEETS

7 PUMPKINS
(5 TO 8 INCHES)
'MIDNIGHT'

2 PUMPKINS (5 INCHES)
'BLACK FOREST
KABOCHA'

7 PUMPKINS
(5 TO 10 INCHES)
'JARRAHDALE'

4 PUMPKINS
(5 TO 8 INCHES)
'TETSUKABUTO'

8 PUMPKINS
(4 TO 6 INCHES)
'CASPERITA'

1 LARGE BUNCH
LACINATO KALE

2 BUNCHES WHEAT
'SILVER TIP'

COLOR PALETTE

| MOSS | MIDNIGHT GREEN | LAUREL GREEN | MISTY | MIRKWOOD | POWDER WHITE |

ADDITIONAL TABLE DECOR

5 NEUTRAL-COLORED TAPER CANDLES
5 WOODEN TAPER CANDLE HOLDERS
1 WOODEN CAKE STAND
1 YARD OF BLUSH-COLORED TULLE
2 TO 4 TABLE SETTINGS

Flower Prep

WHEAT, SQUASH, PUMPKIN

Trim the ends of the wheat and hydrate in cold water. With a little dish soap and warm water, wash the gourds. Dry and set aside until ready to use.

4–6"
COLD

KALE

Spray the kale with cold water and store in the refrigerator until ready to use.

Vase Prep

Fill two short bud vases with cold water. Divide the wheat into two bunches and create 2 bouquets. Trim the stems in 1 bouquet to a medium height and the other to a taller height. Secure the stems of each bouquet with a rubber band. Place each bouquet into a bud vase so the wheat appears to shoot up and out of the vase in all directions. Place bud vases to the side. We will circle back to them in step 6.

Shape

1. Create a frame for your tablescape using the sheet moss. Run a strip of moss down the middle of the table, with pieces overlapping to create a patched green table runner. The shape should feel organic and without clean borders.

Color

2. On the right side of the table, stack 7 gourds (of any and all colors) to form a large mound.

3. Create a pumpkin patch, keeping some of the moss underneath visible. This helps preserve the shape crafted in step 1 and create a design that looks as though it were transplanted from the farm onto the table. Lay the remaining 21 gourds, one on top of another, to create small connecting piles of different sizes and colors.

Depth

4. Add the 5 taper candles in their holders to the outside edges of the pumpkin patch.

5. Place a wooden or rustic-looking cake stand on the left side of the table. Loosely wrap the kale with blush-colored tulle and place atop the cake stand. Allow a trail of tulle to drape over the sides of the stand and onto the table.

6. On the far sides of your pumpkin patch, add the bud vases with the wheat. Place the vase with the taller wheat bunch on the left side and the shorter one on the right.

7. Complete the tablescape by laying place settings to the left and right of center.

DIFFICULTY LEVEL
beginner

SEASON
summer

MOOD
bold

VERDUN

*B*righten your home and satisfy your impulse to run naked through the forest with this bountiful arrangement of chestnut foliage. This way, you get to enjoy nature and be as naked as you like without the risk of a public indecency citation. Beautiful and a bit dangerous, the verdure of each towering branch is adorned with spiked, neon-green chestnut pods. Each stem naturally possesses an element of color and depth, leaving us with the happy task of shaping it to perfection. Clad in green, this arrangement of chestnut glows from within to tell a color story that says, "I don't need twelve different kinds of flowers to be cute. I'm cute all on my own." To that I say, "Yes, yes you are!"

INGREDIENT

8 TALL CHESTNUT BRANCHES (WITH SEEDPODS) 'COLOSSAL'

COLOR PALETTE

NEON GREEN	VERDUN

Flower Prep

Crosscut the stems and
hydrate in warm water.

 DEEP
WARM

Vase Prep

Fill a tall cylindrical vase
with cold water.

Shape & Color

1. Prune 2 branches, separating the lateral stems from the
   main branches. This should create several shorter stems to
   work with.

2. Place the shorter stems (and their original branches) in the
   vase to build a low mound. Keep this shape fairly bushy, as it
   will provide structure for the taller, heavier branches to come.

3. Place 1 branch of medium height left of center and 1 more
   branch on the far left side of the vase. This will create a shape
   that is uneven and taller on the left side.

Depth

4. Add 4 tall branches to the arrangement to create height and
   balance the shape. If the shape is wilder than you desire,
   prune away the foliage until the form takes on a more
   pleasing shape.

151

DIFFICULTY LEVEL
beginner

SEASON
winter

MOOD
festive

EVERGREEN

When the lights are hung and the logs have been yuled, it is that time of year when the world falls in love with evergreens. Transform your space into a land of cheer with a magical hoop of contorted white pine and *Eucalyptus*. Constructed using a metal frame and a few well-placed pillows of chicken wire, this easy-to-build centerpiece is a gorgeous green way to gussy up your tabletop for the glittering festivities of the season.

INGREDIENTS

20 STEMS *PINUS STROBUS* 'CONTORTA' (AKA CONTORTED WHITE PINE)

8 STEMS SEEDED *EUCALYPTUS*

7 PINE CONES

COLOR PALETTE

EVERGREEN   POACHED PEAR   GINGERBREAD

TOOLS

BIND WIRE, GREEN
CHICKEN WIRE
FLORAL CLIPPERS
1 (20-INCH) FLORAL HOOP FRAME
PROTECTIVE GLOVES
WIRE CLIPPERS
ZIP TIES

Flower Prep

PINUS, EUCALYPTUS, PINE CONES

Trim the white pine and the seeded
Eucalyptus stems on a 45-degree
angle. Hydrate in cold water.

 4–6"
COLD

Hoop Prep

Use zip ties to attach 6 to 8 small
chicken wire pillows approximately
4 to 6 inches in diameter onto a
20-inch floral hoop centerpiece
frame. Position the majority of the
chicken wire along the bottom
of the hoop with 2 or 3 pieces
near the upper right sector.

Shape

1. Use bind wire to attach a generous amount of contorted
white pine (about half of the stems) into the chicken wire,
covering three-quarters of the frame. Allow the pine to taper
and thin out around the upper left quarter of the hoop. (But
don't leave it bald. That would just be cruel.)

2. Use the chicken wire to add longer stems of contorted white
pine to punctuate the lower left and upper right sides of the
hoop, creating asymmetry.

---

*Since best flower friends always help each other
practice a little bit of gratitude and have fun,
I have two questions: (1) What is your favorite
holiday memory? (2) Have you heard the
Barbra Streisand version of "Jingle Bells" yet?
If you have not, it's an epic, jolly good time.*

Color

3. Use the *Eucalyptus* to exaggerate the shape and lighten the
color palette. Make an informal triangle with three clusters of
the seeded *Eucalyptus*.

Depth

4. Nestle a cluster of 3 pine cones into the hoop just left of
center. Use the bind wire to attach the pine cones to the hoop.
Position the remaining 4 cones so they appear to be tumbling
down towards the center, with some falling to the outside of
the hoop.

A SEA OF FLOWERS

*Y*ou never know when your big break is going to happen. You should always be ready for the unexpected. I believe the adage goes something like "stay ready, so you don't have to get ready." Sage advice, right?

But what does it mean? Does this proverb propose carrying an art portfolio every day with the hope that some random stranger is going to walk up and say, "Hey, you've got eyebrows, want a job?" Is a "big break" just a combination of timing, talent, and opportunity? When we say "opportunity" do we really mean proximity to a person with power? What are the odds? (Sounds like math . . . no thanks.) If there was a formula for success, I'm sure there would be a far-flung blog about it, a viral meme, or at the very least, an illegible scribble on a bathroom wall somewhere.

In 2014, I was a person who rarely relied on faith, chance, or happenstance as a business strategy. Instead, I regularly relied on my instincts (and leaned into a shameless habit of adding a bit of rouge to my cheeks before asking for a favor). Most of the time, I fell flat on my face, got rejected, or worse, ghosted. Thus, my cynicism over being discovered at a soda shop or while running down a beach in a high-cut one-piece wearing a braided wig. That is . . . until it happened to me.

Before we get into the whodunit of it all, let's first define what a "big break" is. Getting a job as a singing waiter at a restaurant on 51st and Broadway in the middle of Times Square is *not* a big break. That is what happens when you are not extremely specific about your dreams of wanting to sing on Broadway. Nor is your big break winning first place in your sixth grade talent show. Especially if you are the only one in your category. That is called winning by default! Lastly, performing in the non-union bus-and-truck tour of *Click Clack Moo!* is NOT. YOUR. BIG. BREAK. Not if you have to drive the bus and unload the truck while dressed as a duck! That is what happens when your theater career is totally fff—, uh . . . plucked!

I believe many big breaks occur in our lifetime, each one propelling us closer towards a place of visibility and respect—with the desired effect of garnering more offers and better opportunities. We get closer to the freedom to choose who we work with, what we work on, when and where we work. That kind of autonomy comes after years of sacrifice, strategy, and *many* big breaks.

My first big break as a florist came in 2014 when I was living in New York City. I'd recently left grad school and I was working at a flower shop in Brooklyn, selling *Wicked* T-shirts at the Gershwin Theatre, and building my own floral business. I was surfing on a wave of determination. I desperately wanted to make a name for myself as a floral designer. Breaking out in an industry that was not in short supply of experienced florists presented a unique challenge. How do you make a splash when the pool is already full?

After doing a bit of research, I noticed all the florists I'd come to respect were published artists. Their work could be seen in magazines, books, and blogs. So, I set a goal for myself: five years. If I worked hard and made the right connections, maybe I'd get noticed by a magazine editor and have a chance to work with them. If I could get my work featured somewhere prominent, I would have the credibility to elevate my business to a new level: the level that ends with a paycheck instead of a gift card.

Imagine my surprise, horror, and excitement when I got an email asking if I wanted to participate in the cover shoot for the winter issue of *New York* magazine. Let me repeat: The Cover Shoot (I capitalized that so you know it was a big deal). What was I going to do? This was four years ahead of schedule!

I panicked. *Am I ready? I don't feel ready. But I'm not going to let anyone else know that. I'm just going to roll with it, and if they start screaming and call me out for being a no-talent hack, I'll pretend like I was in the wrong place and these ugly flowers are really for someone else!*

The brief from the creative team mentioned that the photographer wanted bridal bouquets in bold monochromatic color palettes. This was a win. Bold monochromatic color palettes were (and still are) my thing. I saw this as a sign that the flower gods were going to be gentle with me. But oh no, they had other plans.

The morning before the shoot, I ventured to the flower market to procure ingredients for two bouquets. I knew I'd have to work fast because all the special flowers were usually scooped up quickly by big floral design houses. Luckily, it was pretty empty that morning, so I didn't need to pull a fire alarm as a distraction while I pillaged the carts of gullible, panicked shoppers.

Almost immediately, I landed on two color palettes: one of deep burgundy with base notes of eggplant and wine and one of vivid yellow, aureolin, and lemon. The darker palette was inspired by a rich and haunting garden rose called 'Gospel'. I'd never seen this rose variety before and it was love at first sight. I was gobsmacked by the deeply ruffled petals and its cupped form. I decided to pair the velvety roses with 'Chocolate Explosion' grass, dark plum mini calla lilies, 'Black Knight' *Scabiosa,* and chocolate *Dahlias.* It was a floral fantasy fit for a first date with a vampire.

The intention behind the yellow bouquet was for it to hum with energy, feeling buoyant and vibrant. I planned to use a flouncy *Oncidium* orchid to add depth to the design. Unlike traditional orchids, this variety has many small florets on long bending stems. I also chose a flirty yellow rose, mustard-yellow *Zinnia,* bright aureolin *Craspedia,* sun-filled pincushion proteas, and buttery 'Beatrice' garden roses. I was thrilled with the effortless movement this bouquet would embody.

I was ready.

With a bundle of flowers under each arm, I made my way to the nearest subway station. Even though I was nearly eaten by a giant raccoon, which was actually just a discarded wig lying on the sidewalk, nothing was going to get me down. I boarded the train feeling confident and ready to begin designing. For the first time since accepting the assignment, I stepped out of my fear and shifted my thoughts in a hopeful direction. I started to believe that I could pull this off. I could do this. Maybe I was ready for this moment. Maybe I wasn't a fraud.

I should have known better than to trust that sticky-sweet feeling of calm.

This is the part of the story where my inexperience shows its innocent, doe-eyed, green face. After spending the rest of the day working and reworking the bouquets until they reached floral perfection, I neglected the number one rule of working with delicate flowers: *Always* store them in a cool place and *never* leave them in the heat.

The thing about New York in late September is that even though it's technically fall, the city holds on to swampy summer weather like a determined subway rat with a piece of pizza. It was so hot you could close your eyes and imagine yourself in the bayou of New Orleans clutching a sweet tea and recalling a night of passion with a hulking man named Brick. Despite the heat and humidity, the dog days of summer in New York are almost romantic . . . until the smell of cooking garbage and urine ransacks your nostrils to destroy the moment and bring you back to reality.

The next morning, both bouquets were so withered and limp they looked more like boiled cabbage than bridal bouquets. I had two hours to deliver the flowers and come up with a plan B. I could swap out the busted stems for the leftovers, but I still wouldn't have enough material to re-create my bouquets. I would have to go back to the flower market and pick up the remaining items.

In less than two hours, I needed to shower, get dressed, pack the bouquets, draw on my eyebrows (so I didn't look like a Black Uncle Fester), get on the subway during rush hour to travel 120 blocks south to purchase new flowers, remake the bouquets, and catch another train across town to the studio with my designs and my eyebrows intact. I took one last look in the mirror and said, "YES. I. CAN!"

NO. I. DID. NOT.

By the time I arrived at the shoot, I was over an hour late and my eyebrows hadn't made it past 96th Street. But the bouquets looked great. I stood outside the studio door, pausing to catch my breath. Looking back, I now realize that I was finding my courage.

Even as doubt and shame turned the voices in my head into a roar—*Turn around! You can't show up this late! You should be embarrassed of yourself!*—the spark inside of me, tiny as it was, said, *Keep going. You made it this far. Of all the florists in the city,* New York *magazine singled you out to be part of this project. Without your flowers, they won't have any bouquets for the shoot. You deserve to cross the finish line. You deserve to be here.*

I timidly opened the door.

Slowly, I entered a massive studio that was completely dark. The only areas that had light were the makeup station at the far end of the room and the set. To my delight, the teams of makeup artists, stylists, set designers, and photography assistants were occupied with their individual tasks and didn't even notice that I'd slipped in. The model's hair was still being finessed as the photographer examined the set and framed his shot.

Less than a moment later, I was greeted by the fashion editor whose calm energy washed over me like cool water over a burn. As she ushered me into the space, I found myself arrested and stunned by what I saw.

A huge section of the floor had been turned into a wild floral installation—a field brimming with luscious vines and clusters of blooms in every color palette imaginable. It was a sea of flowers. Still holding my bouquets, I gravitated towards the magical meadow to examine the garden more closely. My wonderment turned to dread. This was not an installation. This was a massive clump of individual bouquets. This was no sea of flowers. It was a graveyard for my hopes and dreams. But where did they all come from?

Up until that moment I believed that I was the only one asked to provide flowers for this project. It never occurred to me that other florists were asked to provide them too. There was no way all these flowers were going to make it into the final spread. Had I known this was going to be a competition, I would have worn my glittery fanny pack.

What once felt like a great honor turned into a thin-lipped acceptance of a participation ribbon. Devastation crept in as I took in an ocean of floral masterpieces. These bouquets were stunning. Each expertly crafted and curated by what must have been some sort of coalition of floral geniuses who most likely grew and harvested flowers from their palatial cutting gardens in the wealthiest part of Connecticut while drinking two-hundred-year-old bottles of wine to the sounds of Stevie Wonder giving a private concert. There was no way my amateur bouquets were going to stand out among these magnificent offerings.

All I had to do now was add my flowers to the pile and escape the room as soon as possible. I was already fantasizing about which bucket of ice cream I was going to destroy in an attempt to mourn this disaster, when the fashion editor turned to me and said, "Let's go say hi to the photographer."

With bouquets clutched tightly in each arm, I stepped over, around, and through what I'd deemed "flower purgatory" towards the photographer. Upon hearing his name, he turned to look at me with a sweet curiosity that quickly turned into a wide-eyed grin. Had he not noticed that after repeatedly using the cuff of my sleeve to wipe sweat off my forehead that my eyebrows had been smudged up into my hairline? In fact, he hardly looked at my face at all. He seemed to only have eyes for my chest. But it couldn't be that. I hadn't worked out in months. My pecs were flatter than a tone-deaf soprano.

Was he looking at my flowers? He was more than just ogling my bouquets . . . he was *crushing* on them. He had so many questions about the designs, from how I selected the flowers to color choices and more. His genuine fascination for my work began to counter my negative self-talk.

As I stood there, smiling and nodding in agreement, a battle raged inside my head: my inner champion vs. my inner enemy. Though the enemy showed up with fists ablaze, those brief moments of distance helped my inner champion find their voice. They sang a song of absolution. It was an anthem that rebuked catastrophe. The verses said, "Look at how far you have come," and the chorus reminded me to breathe. As the song faded, one final note rang out to say, "I AM ENOUGH."

I could feel the spark from within growing—and it would prove to be more potent and long-lasting than any praise I could have received from the outside. It no longer mattered if they were going to choose me. *I* chose me. The disappointment of not arriving on time melted away. I was going to be okay.

As I turned to add my flowers to the void and make my exit, I heard the photographer say, "Why don't we start with those?" Not wanting to obstruct anyone's view, I moved out of the way. It took a beat to realize he wasn't talking to an assistant. He was talking to me. He was looking at me.

"Let's start with the dark one," he said. I moved with cheetah speed, quickly dried the stems so water would not get on the model's gown, and tied it off with a length of black lace ribbon I'd been keeping in my pocket for the occasion. The energy in the room quickened to an electric rhythm that signaled the shoot was finally about to kick off. I left before the bulbs started flashing. I wouldn't know if they actually used the bouquet until the winter issue arrived.

When I'd gotten word that it was finally available, I had to venture to multiple newsstands and bodegas before I located a copy. When I opened it, there they were. Each of my bouquets had been featured in a separate full-page photo. I must have been dreaming. I felt the world tilt as tears prickled at my eyes. In classic New York City fashion, there was nowhere to sit, so I reached for the nearest rack of potato chips to prop myself up. Once I began to feel my face again, I left the bodega with every copy they had and a few bags of BBQ chips . . . because, well, why not.

In the days that followed, I saw an increase in business inquiries and offers. Many of these jobs came with larger budgets and more artistic freedom. Yes! This was the break I was hoping for. The break I did not expect to receive. The break so big that it would change my life forever.

It turned out to be the break that I gave myself.

You see, somewhere along the way I had become so preoccupied with the notion of what success should *look* like, that I had forgotten what success should *feel* like. I'd spent so much time in the fantasy of my future that I forgot to appreciate the fantasy that I was already in.

The joy of this story isn't the conclusion where we all find out my flowers got published. That's the cherry on top. The cake and all that yummy frosting? You know, the parts that really count? The cake is all that comes before the ending.

The real accomplishment is that after all those mishaps and detours, I still showed up for myself. That the nagging voice inside my head telling me that I should turn around and go home didn't succeed. I kept going. My own persistence proved to me that fear, guilt, and shame only have as much power as I allow them to have.

"Big breaks" only come when you are able to shed the disappointment of dashed expectations—and learn to honor the strength it takes to keep going. Putting one foot in front of the other trains our emotional muscles to keep moving forward when faced with hardships. This is how we become resilient. So, the next time feelings of self-doubt and shame cause you to feel a level of stress so intense that your eyebrows decide to secede from your face, remember to give yourself a break. A big break.

Blue

DIFFICULTY LEVEL
advanced

SEASON
autumn

MOOD
romantic

SKY

*P*icture it: Detroit, summer of 1993. Laying underneath a giant oak tree is a dark-skinned, gap-toothed nine-year-old. He is terrified. As he looks up through a canopy of lush green toward a vast blue sky, he plays a cassette on his Walkman named "The Bodyguard." When the powerful voice of Whitney Houston soars, his soul is lifted into a weightless daydream. There among the clouds he discovers a version of himself that is not afraid to love who he wants or be crippled by the fear of rejection. This avatar is a vision of hope and strength that gives our young protagonist a sense of purpose and belonging. It is only then that the lyrics, *I will always love you* find a home in him. As he descends from the firmament of his fantasy, his feet find purchase on the ground, soft and supporting. He is renewed. Inspired by that day, this arrangement of Dogwood, *Gomphrena,* and *Dahlia* is a piece of that sky.

INGREDIENTS

10 STEMS
BLUE RED-OSIER
DOGWOOD BERRIES

15 STEMS
GOMPHRENA GLOBOSA
'QIS WHITE'

10 STEMS
MINI POMPON *DAHLIA*
'SMALL WORLD'

COLOR PALETTE

KELLY GREEN   SKY BLUE   WHIPPED CREAM   VAPOR

CHICKEN WIRE
FLORAL CLIPPERS
PIN FROG, MEDIUM
PROTECTIVE GLOVES
WATERPROOF FLORAL TAPE
WIRE CUTTERS

Flower Prep

DOGWOOD BERRIES

Trim the dogwood berry stems on a 45-degree angle and hydrate in warm water.

 DEEP WARM

GOMPHRENA

Remove excessive foliage and any laterals from the *Gomphrena* stems. Trim on a 45-degree angle and hydrate in cold water.

 3–5" COLD

DAHLIA

Remove all foliage and any lateral blooms from the *Dahlia* stems. Submerge the stems in water and trim on a 45-degree angle. Immediately hydrate in cold water and store in a floral cooler or refrigerator (see Floral cooler on page 15).

 DEEP COLD

Vase Prep

In a medium-sized compote, add the pin frog and a chicken wire pillow. Secure the chicken wire with a floral tape strap. Fill with cold water.

Shape

1. Separate and divide 6 dogwood berry stems to create 12 to 16 shorter stems. Place these stems in the vase to create a fluffy mound that is wider than it is tall. Allow some foliage and berries to lean out of the side of the vessel, creating a draping effect.

2. Add the remaining 4 tall pieces of dogwood to the arrangement to build out the shape while adding height. Leave plenty of space between the taller dogwood stems to create a shape that is light and airy.

Color

3. Use most of the *Gomphrena* to fill in the gaps and empty spaces left in the lower parts of the arrangement.

4. Balance the taller stems of dogwood placed in step 2 with 2 to 3 tall stems of *Gomphrena*, positioned just left of center and right of center.

Depth

5. Set aside the tallest and curviest *Dahlia* stem.

6. Staying low, add 3 short *Dahlias* to the left side of the arrangement to form a small triangle. Don't forget to rotate and work on the back. Or as my four-year-old son says, "Duh—back!"

7. Use the remaining 6 *Dahlias* to fill in any gaps. Continue to draw the eye upward by placing the final and tallest *Dahlia* set aside in step 5 on the right side of the arrangement.

SAPPHIRE

Who do you think you are?! Well I will tell you: You are a courageous, beautiful, sensitive soul. One whose penchant for the finer things in life has fostered a healthy obsession with the best the earth has to offer: Flowers!

DIFFICULTY LEVEL
advanced

SEASON
winter

MOOD
classic

SAPPHIRE

*B*lue *Hydrangeas* are a treat to have in the home. Their vast color profile gives each head a layered, multidimensional appearance. Each floret is expressive, rich, and varied. When dried properly, this variety can be nearly identical to the freshly cut versions of themselves. So much so that you may not have noticed that the *Hydrangea* in this arrangement are, in fact, dried. Yes, you read that correctly. They are *dried*. I found them tucked underneath a table at the flower market a few months ago. Now they have come out of hiding to take their place among the rest of these glamorous flowers where they belong.

INGREDIENTS

10 STEMS
DRIED *HYDRANGEA*
'NIGRA'

16 STEMS
SCABIOSA CAUCASICA
'PERFECTA BLUE'

24 STEMS
CORNFLOWER
'FOREST BLUE'

COLOR PALETTE

SAPPHIRE

ON THE ROCKS

ROYAL BLUE

Flower Prep

HYDRANGEA

While beautiful, any flower when dried is highly brittle. Store the *Hydrangea* in a traffic-free zone. Once in an arrangement, ① change the water daily to prevent mold and ② immediately remove fresh flowers that have withered. Once all the fresh flowers are gone, dump the water and save your dried beauties for another project. It's the bloom that keeps on giving!

SCABIOSA, CORNFLOWER

Remove all foliage from the *Scabiosa* and cornflower stems. Trim on a 45-degree angle and hydrate in cool water.

 2–4"
COLD

Vase Prep

Add a floral tape grid across the top of a small vase. Secure your grid with a floral tape ring just under the lip of the vase. Fill with cool water.

Shape

1. Set aside the tallest and most expressive *Hydrangea* stem for step 4.

2. Gently place 5 dried *Hydrangea* stems so they drape over the lip of the vase, creating a halo. Trim them fairly short and insert the stems at a nearly horizontal angle.

3. Starting just left of center and working your way to the left, create asymmetry and height with 4 more *Hydrangea* stems.

4. Add the tallest and most expressive stem set aside in step 1 to the left side, drawing the eye upward.

Color

5. Trim 5 *Scabiosa* stems short. Place 1 stem low, to the right of center. Spread the other 4 stems out towards the right side of the arrangement. Though they are supposed to sit low, the *Scabiosa* should be long enough to hover just above the *Hydrangea* and still sit in the water below.

Pro tip

If you cut a *Scabiosa* too short, use a *Hydrangea* like a pillow and rest the head of the *Scabiosa* on top. As long as the stems are long enough to be in water, all is well.

6. With their faces turned front, place 4 *Scabiosa* stems low in each corner of the arrangement.

7. Using the lowest and most central *Scabiosa* as your starting point, add the remaining 7 tall stems that gradually grow in length as they stretch out from the right side of the arrangement.

Depth

8. Use all 24 cornflower stems to fill in gaps, build out the shape, and exaggerate the lines created by the *Scabiosa*. As you go, trim the stems to your desired height—ranging from low to extra tall. Keep most of the cornflower to the right of the arrangement, with only a few stems drifting to the left side.

Pro tip

Reserving most of the *Scabiosa*
and cornflower for one side of the
arrangement allows the eye to
digest color and observe the shape
more easily. If blended too much,
these petite blooms would be lost
amongst the vivacious *Hydrangeas*.

FRENCH BLUE

*I*n recent years, many designers have stopped using *Gypsophila* (aka baby's breath) in their work because it harkens back to an era when flower arrangements collected dust on top of a lace doily next to the bran muffins and a framed photo of Warren Beatty. I don't know what the fuss is about. Warren Beatty used to be the bee's knees, bran muffins are scrummy, and I like baby's breath. I have found the fullness of this bloom perfectly suited for arrangements that need to command the space they occupy. Both *Gypsophila* and *Nigella* have multiple blooms on each stem, letting designers get fuller arrangements using less.

INGREDIENTS

30 STEMS *GYPSOPHILA*
(AKA BABY'S BREATH),
PINK

36 STEMS *NIGELLA*
'MISS JEKYLL

COLOR PALETTE

BABY PINK   FRENCH BLUE

TOOLS

FLORAL CLIPPERS
PROTECTIVE GLOVES

Flower Prep

GYPSOPHILIA

Trim the *Gypsophila* stems
on a 45-degree angle and
hydrate in cold water.

 6–8"
COLD

NIGELLA

Nigella has a ton of small pinlike
leaves that extend all the way up
to the base of the flowering heads.
Leave this foliage on (the impact
of its removal is not worth the
hassle), and gently remove any
foliage that is below the last system
of flowers. Trim on a 45-degree
angle and hydrate in cold water.

 6–8"
COLD

Vase Prep

Fill an extra-large, tall black
urn with cold water.

Shape

1. Gather 12 to 15 stems of pink *Gypsophila* to form a small bouquet. Keep your grip loose and leave the stems as long as possible. Trim the stems until even and place the bouquet into the vase. Zhuzh as needed to form a softly round puff.

2. Working outward from the center, use the remaining stems of *Gypsophila* to build out the shape until it doubles in size, becoming taller and lighter in appearance.

Color & Depth

3. Add 12 stems of blue *Nigella* to the center of the arrangement to mimic the puff created in step 1. Be careful not to break the fragile *Gypsophila* stems as the *Nigella* is added.

4. Use the remaining stems to punch up the color and add dimension to the arrangement.

DIFFICULTY LEVEL
advanced

SEASON
spring

MOOD
romantic

LAPIS

*F*irst things first: Hyacinths are toxic! If you are sensitive to flowers like daffodils and euphorbia, you may want to skip this one. *If you are down for the challenge, wear gloves and avoid touching your face and eyes. Oh, and don't eat it.* I shouldn't have to say that last part, yet here we are. Wash your hands thoroughly when you are done. Beautiful blue shades of hyacinth and tendrils of lustrous *Tradescantia* are dramatically splayed across a gilded divide with clusters of grape hyacinth so dark you could get lost in them. Keep in mind that bendy stems add movement to an arrangement—get ready to be swept away. You've earned it.

INGREDIENTS

15 STEMS HYACINTH 'DELFT BLUE'

10 STEMS HYACINTH 'BLUE JACKET'

40 STEMS *MUSCARI LATIFOLIUM* (AKA GRAPE HYACINTH), DARK BLUE

8 STEMS FROM AN 8- TO 10-INCH POTTED *TRADESCANTIA ZEBRINA* PLANT 'SILVER PLUS'

COLOR PALETTE

| LAPIS | BLUE JACKET | BLUEBERRY | DARK ROYAL PURPLE | BLUE SAGE |

CHICKEN WIRE
FLORAL CLIPPERS
PIN FROG, LARGE
PROTECTIVE GLOVES
WATERPROOF FLORAL TAPE
WIRE CUTTERS

Flower Prep

TRADESCANTIA

Trim greenery from the *Tradescantia* by clipping stems from the plant, ensuring the nodes are intact.

HYACINTH

Hyacinths often come with the whole bulb or part of the bulb attached. Leave the bulbs on and place in cold water until you are ready to arrange. Just before you start with step 1, cut off the bulb and any of the firm white tissue at the bottom of the stem. Hyacinths will absorb water only through the green part of the stem.

MUSCARI

Muscari are short-stemmed flowers. Trim a little off the bottom and hydrate in cold water.

 2–4"
COLD

Vase Prep

In a large pedestal vase, add a large pin frog and a chicken wire pillow. Secure both with a floral tape strap. Fill with water.

Pro tip

Consider the silhouette you want to display when selecting your vessel. For this design, I would use a tall pedestal or urn vase, as it lets the trailing *Tradescantia* effortlessly billow out of the vase.

Shape

1. Starting low, add 5 'Delft Blue' hyacinth stems near the rim of the vase. If the stems have a natural curve, position them to drape out of the vase.

2. With the remaining 10 stems of the lighter blue hyacinth, build out the shape. Use medium and tall stems to fill out the left side to add height and fullness. Leave an evident gap in the middle of the arrangement.

3. Cut 3 'Blue Jacket' hyacinth stems short and place them low in the center towards the front of the vase. Don't forget to do the back too. Place the remaining 2 hyacinth stems low, blending the 2 shades of blue in the arrangement.

4. On the right side, add 4 medium to tall 'Blue Jacket' hyacinth to match the shape created on the left side.

5. Add 1 extra-bendy stem to drape over the edge of the vase.

Color

6. Stay low and use 17 *Muscari* stems to fill in any gaps that may expose your mechanics.

7. Add 15 medium to tall *Muscari* stems to the right side of the vase. The shape should echo the shape created by the tall 'Blue Jacket' hyacinths.

8. Add the remaining 8 *Muscari* stems to the left side of the arrangement. Here, bendy stems are welcome. Place them low so they hang over the lip of the vase.

Depth

9. Place the *Tradescantia* towards the outer edges of your arrangement, allowing its vines to gently tumble over the lip of the vase. Tuck the shorter stems in low and position the longer stems to drape out of the urn.

Pro tip

A little goes a long way. Spread the *Tradescantia* out around the arrangement. The blue sage color really pops against the hues of the hyacinth.

187

A RAINBOW OF ARRANGEMENTS

PERIWINKLE

When I stumbled upon this variety of *Cynoglossum* for the first time, I tripped and fell (in love). Like a flopping fish. I lay on the ground in shock. Eventually, out of mercy, the staff at the flower market had to sweep me away with one of those giant brooms they use to clean up trash at a sports arena. I'm not calling myself "trash," but if you saw the coat I was wearing, you might beg to differ. Matte and bright as a flame, the blue hue of this flower is like nothing I have ever seen. Every one of these luminous blossoms is a standout in this design. The addition of 'Royal Navy' sweet peas helps break up the texture of the *Cynoglossum while* adding depth and beauty. Combined, these two blooms effortlessly enthrall our senses with twinkling visions of periwinkle.

INGREDIENTS

20 STEMS
CYNOGLOSSUM AMABILE
'FIRMAMENT'

20 STEMS SWEET PEAS
'ROYAL NAVY'

COLOR PALETTE

BLUE FLAME · PERIWINKLE

TOOLS

CHICKEN WIRE
FLORAL CLIPPERS
PROTECTIVE GLOVES
WATERPROOF FLORAL TAPE
WIRE CUTTERS

Flower Prep

CYNOGLOSSUM, SWEET PEA

Remove all foliage from all the
stems. Trim on a 45-degree angle
and hydrate in cold water.

2–4"
COLD

Vase Prep

In a small pedestal vase or urn, add
a chicken wire pillow. Secure using
a floral tape strap. Fill with water.

Shape & Color

1. Divide the laterals from 7 longer stems of *Cynoglossum* to
   create many short stems. Pack these short stems closely
   together near the base of the vase to camouflage the
   mechanics.

2. Use 10 medium to tall *Cynoglossum* stems to increase the
   volume and expand the shape of the cloud. Place each
   Cynoglossum at an angle, creating a small valley in the center
   of the arrangement. The left and right sides of the piece
   should reach out and away from each other.

3. Add 3 extra-long *Cynoglossum* stems to the right of center so
   they reach up and out from the right side of the arrangement.

Depth

4. Tuck 4 short sweet peas in the center of the arrangement.
   The stems should be trimmed to sit low, amid the lowest,
   shortest *Cynoglossum*.

5. Fluff out the shape of the arrangement with the remaining
   16 sweet pea stems. On the far-right side of the arrangement,
   create a fan of sweet peas. Mirror this shape on the far-left
   side of the arrangement.

191

DIFFICULTY LEVEL
beginner

SEASON
spring

MOOD
whimsical

ELECTRIC BLUE

*T*he electric blue of these *Violas*, when paired with 'Excelsior Blue' *Hyacinthoides*, creates a jolt of excitement through the body of this frothy, expressive arrangement. Adding a mocha-tinted rose to the mix helps neutralize and balance the fizzing blues radiating from the *Violas*. When it comes to positioning the roses and *Violas*, be sure to face them out so you can enjoy all their ruffled goodness.

INGREDIENTS

6 STEMS GARDEN ROSE 'KOKO LOKO'

16 STEMS *HYACINTHOIDES HISPANICA* 'EXCELSIOR'

20 STEMS *VIOLA* 'FRIZZLE SIZZLE YELLOW-BLUE SWIRL'

COLOR PALETTE

MOCHA   EXCELSIOR BLUE   ELECTRIC BLUE   FRIZZLE SIZZLE   MAHOGANY

Flower Prep

GARDEN ROSE

Remove all thorns and foliage
from the roses. Trim on a
45-degree angle and hydrate
in room temperature water.

 DEEP
ROOM TEMP

HYACINTHOIDES

Trim the *Hyacinthoides*
on a 45-degree angle and
hydrate in cold water.

 2–4"
COLD

VIOLA

Trim the *Violas* on a
45-degree angle and hydrate
immediately in cold water.

 2–4"
COLD

Vase Prep

In the basin of a small pedestal
vase, use floral putty to secure a
round, hairpin floral frog (if you
have one—a standard pin frog will
work as well). Fill with cold water.

Shape

1. Starting low, place 3 rose stems around the circumference
   of the vase. Face them out so the heads rest over the lip of
   the vase.

2. Drape another rose out of the right side of the vase. It should
   fall lower and farther away than the other roses.

3. Add the last 2 rose stems to the arrangement, placing the
   taller rose on the right side and a medium-length rose facing
   out to the left.

Pro tip

'Koko Loko' garden roses can vary in color. In
some instances, they may look golden brown
or even lavender. If you cannot find light
mocha roses, you can substitute with 'Toffee,'
'Golden Mustard,' or 'Cupcake' roses.

Color

4. Fill out the center and the spaces in between the roses using
   11 *Hyacinthoides* stems to create a low, loose bed of flowers.
   Keep the majority of the blooms to the left side. There should
   be visible gaps on the right side to allow space for the *Violas*.

5. Add the remaining 5 stems of *Hyacinthoides* to the vase
   to extend the lines and add volume. Place the tallest stem
   on the left so it dramatically reaches towards the sky. If it
   bends a bit, that is okay! Bending stems bring movement to
   arrangements, making them feel alive.

Depth

6. Position all 20 *Violas* to fill in the spaces left behind by
   the *Hyacinthoides*, with stem heights ranging from low to
   medium. Work from the center outward until the *Violas* reach
   beyond the outer edges of the vase. Resist stuffing them on
   top of each other. A little bit of space between the *Violas* lets
   them breathe, creating depth.

195

Indigo

DIFFICULTY LEVEL
beginner

SEASON
autumn

MOOD
classic

INK

*A*fter the charm of its flowers have faded, *Viburnum* continues to astound with its iridescent, inky-blue berries that glint against matchstick-thin auburn stems. Set against a backdrop of fresh green foliage, this autumnal offering is a stylish way to transition your space away from the chili-pepper reds and sunburnt oranges of summer into the darker, more striking tones of autumn. This long-lasting wreath sustains its beauty even when dried. Finish with velvet and silk ribbons to catapult it from "common adornment" to "classic elegance" everyone will adore.

INGREDIENTS

30 STEMS
VIBURNUM TINUS
'SPRING BOUQUET'

COLOR PALETTE

INK	BRIGHT GREEN

TOOLS

BIND WIRE
FABRIC SCISSORS
FLORAL CLIPPERS
PROTECTIVE GLOVES
6-FOOT-LONG, 2-INCH-WIDE SILK RIBBON
6-FOOT-LONG, 2-INCH-WIDE
VELVET RIBBON
WIRE CLIPPERS
12-INCH SQUARE WREATH FRAME

Flower Prep

Trim the *Viburnum* on a 45-degree angle and hydrate in room temperature water. Store in a floral cooler or refrigerator until ready to use (see Floral cooler on page 15).

 5–7"
ROOM TEMP

Shape

1. Split and divide the *Viburnum* branches into fifteen small bunches, each approximately 3 to 5 inches wide and 6 to 8 inches in length. The square shape of the frame serves as the foundation for this design. Keep the bunches tight to exaggerate this angular shape.

Pro tip

If you have extra energy because you stayed home last night to catch up on your soaps instead of partying with your friends, apply that energy to secure the stems of each small bunch with a bit of bouquet tape to make small posies.

2. Take a length of bind wire, wrap it around the frame, and tie a knot. Do not cut the bind wire from the spool.

Color

3. Position the first bunch of *Viburnum* so it lays along the length of the frame. Secure this bunch to the frame with bind wire from step 2 until attached. Avoid wrapping the berries and the foliage, as this will give the piece a smushed appearance.

4. Lay a second bunch of *Viburnum* onto the frame so the foliage and berries cover the stems of the previously attached bunch. Use the bind wire to secure to the frame. Don't worry if there are still stems poking out. They will become less visible as more bunches are added to the frame.

5. Repeat steps 3 and 4 until the entire frame is covered in *Viburnum*.

6. Attach and tuck the stems of the last bunch underneath the top of the first bunch. Tie a closing knot and snip the end of the bind wire with the wire clippers. Trim the bottoms of any stems that are visible.

Depth

7. Carefully turn the wreath facedown. Gather the velvet and silk ribbons together and fold in half to an even length. Gently use a slipknot to attach the ribbon to the frame. With fabric scissors, trim the ends of the ribbon at a 45-degree angle. Now go and hang that blue beauty somewhere you can enjoy it!

DIFFICULTY LEVEL
advanced

SEASON
winter

MOOD
classic

INDIGO

*T*here are only two "ingredients" in this arrangement. Though it may not sound like enough, when used in abundance two ingredients can easily turn heads and make hearts thump with the kind of adoration and verbal elation typically reserved for a puppy wearing a Sherlock Holmes costume. The success of this arrangement comes down to the flowers. Velvety to the touch, the *Anemone* bloom has deeply saturated petals that beautifully contrast with a blackened button of pollen-rich stamens. Partnering this vivid shade of indigo with the bright green *Geranium* foliage offers a visually arresting combination that is sure to please.

INGREDIENTS

10 STEMS
GERANIUM FOLIAGE
'CHOCOLATE-MINT'

30 STEMS
ANEMONE
'MR. FOKKER'

COLOR PALETTE

FRESH GREEN

INDIGO

TOOLS

CHICKEN WIRE
FLORAL CLIPPERS
PIN FROG, LARGE
PROTECTIVE GLOVES
WATERPROOF FLORAL TAPE
WIRE CLIPPERS

Flower Prep

GERANIUM FOLIAGE, ANEMONE

Trim the *Geranium* and *Anemone* stems on a 45-degree angle and hydrate in cold water. Keep the quickly blooming buds closed by storing them in a floral cooler or refrigerator until ready to use (see Floral cooler on page 15).

4–6"
COLD

Vase Prep

In an extra-large bowl, add a large pin frog and top with a chicken wire pillow. Secure with a floral tape strap. Fill with cold water.

Shape

1. Place 4 short *Geranium* foliage stems in the lower right side of the bowl. Keep the stems fairly short, with some leaves hanging over the side of the vessel. Add 6 medium to tall *Geranium* foliage stems to the left side of the bowl. Be sure to leave plenty of empty space in the middle of the arrangement.

Color

2. Set aside the tallest, most expressive *Anemone* stem for step 5. Starting low and near the opening of the vase, place 8 short-cropped *Anemone* stems to fill in any empty spaces around the foliage. Position the outermost blooms to face front and gently hang over the edge of the bowl.

3. Intensify the color by adding 8 *Anemone* stems of medium length in and around the center of the arrangement. Use the pin frog to help position the stems to face out.

4. Use an additional 7 stems to slightly increase the height and widen the shape.

Depth

5. Create depth by adding 6 tall *Anemone* stems on the right side of the arrangement. Place the tallest, final *Anemone* on the right side of the arrangement to draw the eye upward.

6. Make small adjustments to the arrangement by pulling stems near the front out to float from the main crowd of blooms. Creating a layer of flowers that float away from the source while allowing others to remain recessed in shadow creates an impactful field of depth.

205

A RAINBOW OF ARRANGEMENTS

MUSETTA

A house is not a home
until it has flowers.

MUSETTA

*I*nspiration for this piece came from a giant shallow bowl. Sleek and cool in its matte white form, it whispered a promise of blooms rising from a pool of radiant azure. Delicate veins of curly willow effortlessly wind their way through the monochromatic spires of *Aconitum* and *Delphinium* in a spellbinding way. Alone, the flowers used in this piece may feel simple. Together, the final composition is as bold as an operatic aria and as enchanting as a waltz.

INGREDIENTS

10 STEMS	7 STEMS	5 STEMS	5 STEMS
ACONITUM CARMICHAELII 'ARENDSII'	*DELPHINIUM* 'BLUE BIRD'	*PENNISETUM ALOPECUROIDES* 'MOUDRY'	CURLY WILLOW TIPS

COLOR PALETTE

AZURE	BLUEBIRD	RAVEN	SADDLE BROWN

FLORAL CLIPPERS
PIN FROG, LARGE
PROTECTIVE GLOVES
WATERPROOF FLORAL TAPE

Flower Prep

ACONITUM, PENNISETUM

Remove all foliage from the *Aconitum* stems. Trim the *Aconitum* and *Pennisetum* stems on a 45-degree angle and hydrate in cold water.

 5–7"
COLD

DELPHINIUM

Remove all foliage from the *Delphinium* stems. Trim on a 45-degree angle and hydrate in cold water. Store in a cool area, floral cooler, or refrigerator until ready to use (see Floral cooler on page 15).

 4–6"
COLD

CURLY WILLOW

Trim the curly willow stems on a 45-degree angle and hydrate in room temperature water.

 DEEP
ROOM TEMP

Vase Prep

I used a ceramic flower frog bowl (11 inches wide by 3 inches tall) for this piece, but you can make your own version with a large pin frog and a go-getter attitude. Secure a wide 3- to 5-inch pin frog into the center of a large shallow bowl, such as a pie plate or serving dish. Fill with water.

Shape

1. Set aside the tallest, most expressive *Aconitum* stem for step 3. Starting low, cluster 3 short *Aconitum* stems on the left of the frog. On the opposite side of the frog, place 2 more *Aconitum* stems to face outward. There should be a visible empty space in the middle of the vessel.

2. Build out the shape with 4 *Aconitum* stems of medium length positioned on the left side of the frog. This should create an uneven, asymmetrical triangular shape.

3. Add the final *Aconitum* stem to reach up and out of the left side of the floral frog.

4. Use 7 *Delphinium* stems to exaggerate the shape. When trimming, keep the stems at a longer length so the buds reach higher than the low *Aconitum* cluster.

Color

5. Place 5 *Pennisetum* stems on the right side of the floral frog, mirroring the shape created on the left with the *Delphinium*. Start low with 2 or 3 stems cropped close to the frog. Gradually increase the height of the remaining *Pennisetum* until the tallest piece reaches up and out from just right of center.

Depth

6. Add the 5 curly willow tips all over. Position the branches to emphasize and punctuate the shape rather than overwhelm it with texture. This is achieved by keeping the stems on the right fairly low, while the stems on the left reach out and up as they stretch towards the sky.

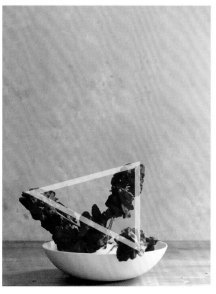

DIFFICULTY LEVEL
beginner

SEASON
summer

MOOD
alluring

NEBULA

*A*s a child, I was obsessed with outer space. Films like *Explorers,
SpaceCamp,* and *Mom and Dad Save the World* made blasting off into
the galaxy look thrilling. Once I found out that I would need a mastery of all
things mathematical to become an astronaut in real life, that dream fizzled out
faster than an open can of pop. Considering that I used a calculator to punch
the numbers 80085 more than I used it for math, I decided to set my dreams of
swimming in the Milky Way aside to reach for something simpler and grounded
in reality: *Broadway!* This bouquet's galactic hues of ultraviolet, deep-space blue,
and liseran purple are a salute to every little boy, girl, and gender nonconforming
kid out there still dreaming of the cosmos.

INGREDIENTS

5 STEMS
TRACHELIUM CAERULEUM
'BLACK KNIGHT'

16 STEMS
ECHINOPS RITRO (AKA
GLOBE THISTLE)
'VEITCH'S BLUE'

16 STEMS
CLARY SAGE
'BLUE MONDAY'

12 STEMS
*VERONICASTRUM
VIRGINICUM*
'PINK GLOW'

COLOR PALETTE

ULTRAVIOLET   DEEP-SPACE BLUE   TRUE
PURPLE   PINK GLOW

TOOLS

BOUQUET TAPE
FLORAL CLIPPERS
PROTECTIVE GLOVES
DECORATIVE RIBBON (OPTIONAL)
FABRIC SCISSORS (OPTIONAL)

Flower Prep

TRACHELIUM, ECHINOPS

Remove all foliage from the
Trachelium and *Echinops*.
Trim on a 45-degree angle
and hydrate in cold water.

4–6"
COLD

CLARY SAGE

Remove any foliage from the clary
sage that will be in the water in
the final arrangement. Trim on a
45-degree angle and hydrate in
cold water. Store in a floral cooler
or refrigerator until ready to use
(see Floral cooler on page 15).

2–4"
COLD

VERONICASTRUM

Remove all foliage from the
Veronicastrum. Trim on a 45-degree
angle and hydrate in cold water.

4–6"
COLD

Shape

1. Gather all 5 *Trachelium* stems to form a soft, round cloud.

Color

2. Working from the lower left side towards the upper right
   corner, add 12 *Echinops* stems to the bouquet. The *Echinops*
   should float slightly above the *Trachelium*.

3. Add the remaining 4 *Echinops* stems to the upper left side
   of the bouquet as if they were the bouncy antennae of an
   adorable alien.

Depth

4. Add most of the clary sage to the right side of the bouquet,
   with a few stems reaching off to the left side of the bouquet.

5. Add all 12 *Veronicastrum* stems to the bouquet, positioned so
   they reach out in all directions.

6. Finish by securing the stems with bouquet tape. Trim the
   ends of the stems until even and place in a vase of cold water
   until ready to use.

Optional

Add a ribbon of your choice. Use fabric
scissors to trim the ends of the ribbon at a
45-degree angle (see Ribbon on page 28).

Pro tip

Echinops foliage is surprisingly sharp.
Wear gloves.

MIDNIGHT

O h hellebore, why can't I quit you? I have a love/hate relationship with hellebores. Well, it's more like a love/why-won't-you-love-me-back relationship. No matter how troublesome these flowers can be, no matter how many times they wilt, no matter how costly they are, I still come running back for more. My practical side loves the simplicity of its single-petal form. My designer side sees an opportunity to create an arrangement in a spellbinding shade of midnight blue. While other arrangements can tower, this piece is only about 10 inches high. Thanks to a lovely combination of hellebore, *Muscari,* and pussy willow, this petite arrangement will make a big impression in any space.

INGREDIENTS

6 STEMS FROM A
POTTED *PEPEROMIA*
PLANT 'LUNA GREY'

30 STEMS
MUSCARI ARMENIACUM
'VALERIE FINNIS'

12 STEMS
FRENCH PUSSY WILLOW,
SILVER

15 STEMS
HELLEBORE
'NEW YORK KNIGHT'

COLOR PALETTE

LUNA
GREY

ALICE'S BLUE

SILVER

MIDNIGHT BLUE

Flower Prep

PEPEROMIA

Trim greenery from the *Peperomia* by clipping stems from the plant, ensuring the nodes are intact.

MUSCARI, FRENCH PUSSY WILLOW

Trim the *Muscari* and pussy willow on a 45-degree angle and hydrate in cold water. Store the *Muscari* in a cool area and keep out of direct sunlight.

 2–4"
COLD

HELLEBORE

Select mature hellebore stems that have developed a bulbous seedpod. Mature hellebores have a longer vase life. Remove any foliage below the last system. Trim the stems on a 45-degree angle while submerged in water in a sink or bucket (this helps prevent air from entering and drying out the stems) and immediately hydrate in cold water. Store the hellebore in a cool area and keep out of direct sunlight.

 4–6"
COLD

Vase Prep

Use something similar to the pinch bowl pictured here, which is only 3½ inches in diameter. Place a small pin frog in the center. Create a floral tape grid along the top of the vase.

Shape

1. Place 5 stems of *Peperomia* around the lip of the vase. Crop them closely so the leaves hang over the edge. On the left side of the vase, add 1 additional long stem that stretches out and down to the left.

Color

2. Place 21 *Muscari* stems to the left of center to create a small cluster. The dome should spill over the left side of the vase. Add another 5 short stems of *Muscari* to the right side of the vase. Keep these stems separated from one another.

3. Add 1 long *Muscari* stem to the right of center so it reaches out and up to the right.

4. Continue to build height by adding 2 tall stems to the left side of the vase and the final tall stem to the back right side.

Depth

5. Starting left of center, build out the height and add texture with all 12 pussy willow stems. The pussy willow should be trimmed to sit taller than the *Muscari*.

6. Nestle 1 short hellebore stem low and to the right of center.

7. Using 7 hellebore stems, build a small dome on the right side of the vase. This shape should mirror the lowest cluster of *Muscari* on the left.

8. Create height on the right side of the arrangement by adding the last 4 tall stems of hellebore.

9. Pepper in 3 hellebore stems on the left side of the arrangement so a hint of color peeks through the *Muscari*.

HAUNTED
HEART

Though flowers do not use words, they still speak to us. The gentle bend of a stem or the crinkle of a leaf tells a story. Our work with nature allows us to share the story of another life through our art.

DIFFICULTY LEVEL
beginner

SEASON
spring

MOOD
whimsical

HAUNTED HEART

When the blooms of the bearded iris are in bud form, they are without question, well, how do I put this kindly... they're ugly. How can something so beautiful start out looking like the thumb of a witch? My apologies if you are an actual witch. I'm sure your thumbs are lovely. (Please don't hex me!) The magic of this arrangement happens when the shriveled, waxy bud of the bearded iris transforms from a creature-of-the-night into a billowing bloom of cascading princess ruffles. Available in unconventional hues like mustard, sepia, and silver blue, the bearded iris just might become your new favorite flower.

INGREDIENTS

10 STEMS FLOWERING
ANTHRISCUS SYLVESTRIS
'RAVENSWING'

15 STEMS BEARDED IRIS
'HAUNTED HEART'

COLOR PALETTE

LONDON GRAY

MAGIC FOG

CHICKEN WIRE
FLORAL CLIPPERS
PIN FROG, LARGE
PROTECTIVE GLOVES
WATERPROOF FLORAL TAPE
WIRE CLIPPERS

Flower Prep

ANTHRISCUS

Gently remove all foliage
from the fragile *Anthriscus*.
Trim on a 45-degree angle
and hydrate in cold water.

4–6"
COLD

BEARDED IRIS

Bearded irises have multiple buds on
each stem, with the top bud maturing
first. The remaining buds bloom as
the mature flowers begin to wilt.
To conserve energy, trim away the
ancillary buds leaving the top flower
intact. Remove any remaining foliage.
Trim on a 45-degree angle and
hydrate in room temperature water.

6–8"
ROOM TEMP

Vase Prep

In a short cylindrical vase, add a
large pin frog and a chicken wire
pillow. Secure with a floral tape
strap. Fill with fresh water.

Shape

1. Use 8 medium-length *Anthriscus* stems to create a loose dome
   just above the lip of the vase. I mean it when I say *loose*. Avoid
   a tight shape. Take a breath and embrace imperfections.

2. Add the remaining 2 stems of *Anthriscus* to the left side
   of the arrangement. Keep the stems long. This height and
   asymmetry will help balance the heavy bearded iris without
   adding bulk.

Color & Depth

3. Trimmed short to sit low in the vase, place 1 bearded iris to
   the right of center. The head should float approximately
   1 to 2 inches above your chicken wire pillow.

4. Use 10 bearded iris stems to mimic the loose dome created by
   the *Anthriscus* and to fill in any spaces and expand the shape
   of the dome.

5. To add height and dimension to the piece, keep the remaining
   4 bearded irises tall and place them in the arrangement.
   Starting on the outer right corner, create a shape that fans out
   and continues to the left side of the arrangement. The tallest
   of the stems should be placed slightly right of center.

*Lastly, exhale. Now grab an Earl Grey tea,
play Dame Cleo Laine, and enjoy the
London fog.*

Remember, imperfect flowers are exciting flowers.

Violet

DIFFICULTY LEVEL
beginner

SEASON
summer

MOOD
whimsical

ENGLISH VIOLET

*T*his sophisticated color palette is a fairy tale. Instead of a young maiden, we have a young color maturing from its bubblegum-pink adolescence into a beguiling shade of lavender. Faintly tinged with hints of English violet, the 'Moonstone' China aster and 'Blue Pompon' roses articulate a fable character ripe with ambition. The bulky asters and roses do most of the work, creating a dazzling shape that comes together quickly. The exuberant *Anemone* elevates this arrangement of understated beauty into a sparkling work of art fit for a queen.

INGREDIENTS

10 STEMS
CHINA ASTER
'MOONSTONE'

7 STEMS
SPRAY ROSE
'BLUE POMPON'

3 STEMS
GOMPHRENA GLOBOSA
'QIS PINK'

17 STEMS
JAPANESE *ANEMONE*
'HONORINE JOBERT'

COLOR PALETTE

ENGLISH VIOLET   MOUNTBATTEN PINK   PINKY LAVENDER   PEARLY PINK

TOOLS

BOUQUET TAPE
FLORAL CLIPPERS
PROTECTIVE GLOVES
DECORATIVE RIBBON (OPTIONAL)
FABRIC SCISSORS (OPTIONAL)

Flower Prep

CHINA ASTER

Remove all foliage and separate any lateral blooms from the aster stems. Trim on a 45-degree angle and hydrate in cold water. Sustain their cupped form by storing them in a refrigerator or allow them to open by leaving them at room temperature.

6–8"
COLD

SPRAY ROSE

Remove any thorns and foliage from the rose stems. Trim on a 45-degree angle and hydrate in room temperature water.

DEEP
ROOM TEMP

GOMPHRENA

Remove all foliage and any lateral blooms from the *Gomphrena* stems. Trim on a 45-degree angle and hydrate in cold water.

4–6"
COLD

JAPANESE ANEMONE

This flower variety does not like the heat and its delicate stems break easily. Gently remove all foliage, keeping the buds nearest to the main bloom attached. Trim on a 45-degree angle and hydrate in cold water.

2–4"
COLD

Shape

1. Use all 10 aster stems to create an uneven, lumpy cloud with a few stems pulled forward and a few tucked deeper into the bouquet. The shape should be dynamic, not flat or smooth. Create asymmetry by positioning 1 stem in the upper left corner and another in the lower right corner.

Color

2. Build out the shape and intensify the color by adding 4 of the spray rose stems to the bouquet. Add the remaining 3 roses to fill in the gaps left by the asters in step 1.

Depth

3. Add the 3 *Gomphrena* stems to the outer left side of the bouquet. These should look as though they are sprouting from the arrangement.

4. Carefully add 14 Japanese *Anemone* stems, working from the center towards the outer right side of the bouquet. The outermost stems should float a few inches away from the core of the bouquet.

5. Add the remaining 3 Japanese *Anemone* stems to the lower left side of the bouquet. Position them to reach out and down, creating asymmetry.

6. Finish by securing the stems with bouquet tape. Trim the stems until even. Hydrate in a vase of cold water until ready to use.

Optional

Add a ribbon of your choice. Use fabric scissors to trim the ends of the ribbon at a 45-degree angle (see Ribbon on page 28).

DIFFICULTY LEVEL
beginner

SEASON
summer

MOOD
playful

DANCING LADIES

*P*etite as a petit four, this small bouquet is big with color. The deeply ruffled blooms in hues of purpureus and eminence embody the playful allure of dancers performing the cancan. Flirty *Violas* and cheerful *Scabiosa* burst into view with contagious joie de vivre. A timeless composition sure to melt the heart of any floral enthusiast, this bouquet is an effortless way to transform any moment into a jubilant celebration.

INGREDIENTS

10 STEMS *VIOLA* 'HALO VIOLET'

15 STEMS SWEET PEA 'DARK PASSION'

5 STEMS *ASTRANTIA MAJOR* 'STAR OF ROYALS'

6 STEMS *SCABIOSA* 'LAVENDER SCOOP'

COLOR PALETTE

PURPUREUS

EMINENCE

SILVER LAKE

AUDRA

BOUQUET TAPE
FLORAL CLIPPERS
PROTECTIVE GLOVES
DECORATIVE RIBBON (OPTIONAL)
FABRIC SCISSORS (OPTIONAL)

Flower Prep

VIOLA

Trim the *Viola* stems on a
45-degree angle and immediately
hydrate in cold water.

 2–4"
COLD

SWEET PEA, ASTRANTIA, SCABIOSA

Trim the sweet pea, *Astrantia*, and
Scabiosa stems on a 45-degree
angle and hydrate in cold water.

 4–6"
COLD

Shape

1. Gather all 10 *Viola* stems to make a loose bundle.

Color

2. Add all 15 sweet pea stems to make a softly round purple cloud.

Depth

3. Pepper the 5 *Astrantia* stems throughout the bouquet.

4. Working across a diagonal, add the 6 *Scabiosa* stems so they travel from the upper left and right corners to the lower left and right corners.

5. Finish by securing the stems with bouquet tape. Trim the stems until even. Hydrate in a vase of cold water until ready to use.

Optional

Add a ribbon of your choice. Use fabric
scissors to trim the ends of the ribbon at a
45-degree angle (see Ribbon on page 28).

235

DIFFICULTY LEVEL
expert

SEASON
spring

MOOD
romantic

HELIOTROPE

*T*his is one of my favorite pieces in this book. What I love is how untamed this arrangement feels while remaining romantic and artful in its design. Let the sinuous *Verbascum* blooms play with each other—the more fun you have, the more dynamic this piece will become. Start the party by positioning flutes of jewel-toned *Delphinium* and zigzagging *Verbascum* to appear as though they are bursting from a mosh pit of fluorescent foliage. We then turn this party into a rave with *Violas* in euphoric hues of mariposa. It is best to meet the challenge of this expert arrangement with a lithe attitude and a playlist packed with bangers.

INGREDIENTS

| 18 STEMS *DELPHINIUM* 'ASTOLAT' | 6 STEMS NINEBARK FOLIAGE 'DART'S GOLD' | 6 STEMS GARDEN ROSE 'DISTANT DRUM' | 16 STEMS *VERBASCUM X HYBRIDA,* 'SOUTHERN CHARM' | 12 STEMS VIOLA 'MARIPOSA' |

COLOR PALETTE

ASTOLAT   BITTER LIME   PALE APRICOT   SOUTHERN CHARM   MARIPOSA

TOOLS

CHICKEN WIRE
FLORAL CLIPPERS
PIN FROG, LARGE
PROTECTIVE GLOVES
WATERPROOF FLORAL TAPE
WIRE CUTTERS

Flower Prep

DELPHINIUM, GARDEN ROSE, VERBASCUM

Remove all foliage from the garden rose, and *Verbascum*. Remove thorns from the roses. Trim on a 45-degree angle and hydrate in room temperature water.

4–6"
ROOM TEMP

NINEBARK, VIOLA

Trim the ninebark and *Viola* stems on a 45-degree angle and hydrate in cold water. Store in a cool area, floral cooler, or refrigerator until ready to use (see Floral cooler on page 15).

2–4"
COLD

Vase Prep

In a tall pedestal (around 6½ inches tall by 8 inches wide), place a large pin frog. Secure a chicken wire pillow atop the pin frog with a floral tape strap. Try to select a vase of a soft shade such as champagne or blush.

Shape

1. Working from the outside of the vase towards the center, add 15 'Astolat' *Delphinium* stems of medium to tall height. Use the stems to make 2 crescent-shaped fans. Leave a sizable gap in the middle of the arrangement.

2. Trim the last 3 *Delphinium* stems to a short length. Place them low to fill the empty space in the middle of the vase, connecting the fans of *Delphinium*. Leave enough room front and center for the garden roses in steps 5 and 7.

Color

3. Increase the number of stems of the ninebark by cutting the lengthy stems into smaller pieces (about 5 to 7 inches each).

4. Staying low and near the lip of the vase, add a pop of color and fill the empty spaces with 6 short ninebark stems. Position the prettiest tips in the visible areas. Pull the color through the rest of the arrangement by tucking the rougher-looking ninebark into the less visible holes and gaps.

Depth

5. Plug 1 garden rose into the open space at the front of the vase.

6. Trimming as you go, so stem heights range from short to tall, place 16 *Verbascum* stems all over the arrangement. Position the blooms so the flowers appear to be shooting out from the center of the arrangement in every direction.

7. Cluster the remaining 5 garden roses together, next to the single rose from step 5. Don't forget to rotate the vase and get the other side!

Okay, flower friend! We are nearly there. It's time to turn up the music and get your selfie face ready because you're going to want to document this one when you're done. (Then tag me on social media @kristengvy, because I wanna see!)

8. Working across the lower third of the arrangement, add all 12 *Viola* stems. Do not stuff these shorties into the arrangement. Maximize their impact by situating the heads of the flowers to face front. This creates a contrast between the vibrant, tangelo-tinged *Violas* and the vivid hues of violet.

DIFFICULTY LEVEL
beginner

SEASON
spring

MOOD
bold

LILAC

O ne magical afternoon, with my trusty clippers in hand, these blooming *Rhododendron* were foraged from . . . okay, this is where the story *should* continue on to say "a hidden grove of cotton candy-colored shrubs that stretched as far as the eye could see." But, nope. These branches were snipped from a potted plant I purchased from a local nursery. When flower love runs deep, it does not matter how a bloom finds its way to your home. The magic is what you do with it. Inspired by their undisturbed form in nature—tumbling and heavy with large spherical clusters of vivid floral—I adopted a modern aesthetic for this piece, using asymmetry to create a moment of singular beauty.

INGREDIENTS

**6 BRANCHES
BLOOMING
RHODODENDRON
'PJM ELITE'**

COLOR PALETTE

LILAC   HUNTER GREEN

Flower Prep

Whether you're harvesting from
a plant or sourcing already cut
stems from a supplier, crosscut
the *Rhododendron* and hydrate
in deep, warm water.

 DEEP
WARM

Vase Prep

Fill a tall and narrow vase (around
18 inches tall with a 4-inch-wide
opening) with room temperature
water. An arrangement with heavy
branches in a big vase full of water
is cumbersome to transport. Build
this piece where it is going to live to
minimize the risk of a floral faux pas.

Shape & Color

1. Divide 1 large *Rhododendron* branch into 3 to 5 short pieces.
   Place these stems into the vase to create a small circular puff
   of flowers. This will help weigh down the vase and create a
   natural armature to support taller, heavier stems.

2. Add 3 branches of medium height to intensify and build the
   shape up and out, widening it. Be sure to balance the stems
   and their weight.

Depth

3. Add the 2 remaining branches. On the left, add a curved
   branch so it appears to cascade out of the vase. On the right,
   add the tallest branch so it appears to be reaching in the
   opposite direction.

DIFFICULTY LEVEL
advanced

SEASON
summer

MOOD
romantic

MAUVE

*M*auve. Yeesh! What a divisive color. Whatever you do, do not talk about mauve when your relatives are around. Especially if the cousin who always wears that MAKE MAUVE GREAT AGAIN hat is there. They have got to stop pushing those unfounded color theories. Some believe that mauve is a sort of brownish-pink color. For others, mauve is a lavenderish tan. The cynic believes mauve is just an elitist way of saying beige. You know, I have spent a lot of time not thinking about this. I have come to believe that—through decades of no research and zero hours of scientific study—mauve is a dusty lavender with barely there pink undertones. If I put it on social media, it'll make it true, right?

INGREDIENTS

18 STEMS GARDEN ROSE
'STEPHEN RULO'

5 STEMS *DAHLIA*
'DOWNHAM ROYAL'

25 STEMS SWEET PEA
'NIMBUS'

13 STEMS CORNFLOWER
'CLASSIC MAGIC'

COLOR PALETTE

MAUVE   DARK MAGENTA   MULBERRY   VOODOO

TOOLS

CHICKEN WIRE
FLORAL CLIPPERS
PIN FROG, LARGE
PROTECTIVE GLOVES
WATERPROOF FLORAL TAPE
WIRE CUTTERS

Flower Prep

GARDEN ROSE

Remove all foliage and thorns
from the rose stems. Trim on
a 45-degree angle and hydrate
in room temperature water.

DEEP
ROOM TEMP

DAHLIA

Remove all foliage and any
laterals branching from the *Dahlia*
stems. Trim on a 45-degree angle
and hydrate in cold water.

4–6"
COLD

SWEET PEA, CORNFLOWER

Remove all foliage and trim the
sweet pea and cornflower stems on
a 45-degree angle and hydrate in
cool water. Store in a cool area, floral
cooler, or refrigerator until ready to
use (see Floral cooler on page 15).

2–4"
COLD

Vase Prep

In a medium-sized footed bowl,
add the pin frog and chicken
wire pillow. Secure with a floral
tape strap. Fill with cold water.

Shape

1. Crop the stems of 12 garden roses short and place in the
   vase to shape a lumpy, uneven mound, with the left side
   sitting slightly higher than the right. Cover any mechanics by
   positioning some of the flowers so their heads hang over the
   lip of the vase, while others fill the space in the middle.

2. On the left, add height and broaden the shape with 4 more
   roses. The addition of the tallest rose should transform the
   shape of the arrangement into an asymmetrical cloud.

3. To the right of center, add the final 2 roses to lean towards the
   right side of the vase. These stems should be cut to medium
   and tall lengths.

Color

4. Working from the center out towards the right, use all
   5 *Dahlias* (of short to medium length) to fill in the gaps and
   bulk up the right side of the arrangement.

Depth

5. Set aside the longest sweet pea stem for step 9. Place 7 short
   sweet pea stems below the bed of roses, as if they were ruffles
   of a petticoat peeking out from underneath a skirt. Keep in
   mind that sweet peas have fragile hollow stems. Be gentle as
   you incorporate them into this arrangement.

6. Sprinkle all 13 cornflower stems (ranging from medium
   height to tall) into the arrangement. Trim the stems as you
   go, ensuring the cornflowers gradually grow in height as they
   stretch towards the right side of the vase. The tallest stem
   should not reach beyond the highest *Dahlia*. Create depth by
   positioning the heads of the cornflowers to face out.

7. Now it is time to bring the drama! Keep clear of the center.
   Work along the outer left and right sides of the arrangement.
   On the left, focus the bulk of the remaining sweet peas
   (about 11 of the remaining 17 stems) to create a shape that
   dramatically fans out and elongates the shape upward.

8. On the right, loosely position 6 sweet pea stems to reach and
   stretch in all directions.

9. Place the last and tallest stem (set aside in step 5) to reach up
   and out from the right side of the arrangement, creating an
   asymmetrical tableau.

247

DIFFICULTY LEVEL
expert

SEASON
spring

MOOD
drama queen

PERSEPHONE

*I*nspired by the mythological Greek goddess of spring and Hades's reluctant queen, this arrangement is the color story of the ingenue Persephone crossing the River Styx into the underworld. Abundant with soft pink droplets of *Aquilegia* and mountains of fragrant lilacs, the mirrored halves of this arrangement are divided by a river of velvety *Scabiosa*. As the lights of the world she has known begin to fade away, our mistress of spring turns her gaze away from the candy-coated pastels of the season to embrace the violet shadows of night.

INGREDIENTS

10 STEMS
LILAC 'MONGE'

28 STEMS
SCABIOSA ATROPURPUREA
'BLACK KNIGHT'

25 STEMS
AQUILEGIA VULGARIS
(AKA COLUMBINE)
'PINK PETTICOAT'

COLOR PALETTE

POMPADOUR PURPLE   MURASAKI PEPPER   RICE   THULIAN PINK

TOOLS

CHICKEN WIRE
FLORAL CLIPPERS
PIN FROG, MEDIUM
PROTECTIVE GLOVES
WATERPROOF FLORAL TAPE

Flower Prep

LILAC

Crosscut the lilac stems and
hydrate in warm water.

6–8"
WARM

SCABIOSA

Remove all foliage and any
laterals branching off the *Scabiosa*
stems. Trim on a 45-degree angle
and hydrate in cold water.

2–4"
COLD

AQUILEGIA

Remove all foliage from the
Aquilegia. Trim on a 45-degree
angle and hydrate in cold water.
Store in a cool area, floral cooler,
or refrigerator until ready to use
(see Floral cooler on page 15).

2–4"
COLD

Vase Prep

In a large (preferably black)
pedestal vase, add a large pin frog
and a chicken wire pillow. Secure
the chicken wire with a floral
tape strap. Fill with cold water.

Shape

1. Start with 5 lilac stems for the left side of the arrangement
and 5 stems for the right side. Keeping the center completely
clear of blooms, use the lilacs to form 2 large sprays of flora
that swell and crest in opposite directions.

Pro tip

Lilacs can be temperamental and wilt with the
slightest provocation. Give any wilting stems a
crosscut and hydrate in deep hot water. For best
results, immediately place the freshly trimmed
stems into a cool area, floral cooler, or refrigerator
(see Floral cooler on page 15).

2. Set aside 1 very tall *Scabiosa* stem for step 4. Use 11 short
Scabiosa stems to fill the space in the middle of the vessel.
Trim the stems to slightly varying heights as you go, so the
construction looks like dark rapids.

Color

3. Add 10 *Scabiosa* stems of varying length to both sides of the
arrangement. Continue to keep the airspace above the central
cluster of *Scabiosa* clear and keep them shorter than the lilac.

4. With 6 *Scabiosa*, emphasize the spray of lilac on the right side.
Trim as you go so the stems range from medium to tall in
height. Place the *Scabiosa* stem set aside in step 2 just to the
right of center. This tall stem should reach towards the sky
(or, in this case, Mount Olympus).

Depth

5. Starting low and staying clear of the center, add 10 *Aquilegia*
stems. Create depth by trimming the stems to different
heights as you go, keeping them long enough to float beyond
the body of the arrangement.

6. Place 1 or 2 *Aquilegia* stems of medium length in the center.
Make sure the blooms do not obscure the river of black
Scabiosa.

7. Trim the remaining 13 or 14 *Aquilegia* as you go, so they range
in height from medium to tall. Position the stems all over the
arrangement, working from the center outward. Allow the
heads of the flowers to float beyond the arrangement. With a
slight gap still evident between the lilac halves, the *Aquilegia*
should balance the piece.

Gentle reminder: Be patient with yourself. No matter your skill level, this is a challenging design with a lot of stem insertions.

DIFFICULTY LEVEL
advanced

SEASON
spring

MOOD
energetic

BYZANTIUM

*W*hether singing in a choir, applying eyeshadow, or standing still in the shadows of your garden to escape a close-talking neighbor, blending has many wonderful uses. As each element is added to this luscious, flamboyant bouquet: *Blend.* Then *blend* some more. The key is to spread the goods out evenly, like dollar bills at a drag show. Here we blend small textured fritillaries and coral-hued roses with parakeet green buttonbush for a polyphony of floral bliss.

INGREDIENTS

5 STEMS *BERZELIA LANUGINOSA* (AKA BUTTONBUSH), GREEN

5 STEMS GARDEN ROSE 'ROMANTIC ANTIKE'

16 STEMS *FRITILLARIA MELEAGRIS* (AKA SNAKE'S HEAD FRITILLARY)

9 STEMS HELLEBORE 'PINK LADY'

8 STEMS BUTTERFLY RANUNCULUS 'HERA'

3 STEMS *FRITILLARIA PERSICA* (AKA PLUM BELLS FRITILLARY)

COLOR PALETTE

| PARAKEET | CORAL | BYZANTIUM | PINK LADY | TAFFY | WINE O'CLOCK |

TOOLS

BOUQUET TAPE
FLORAL CLIPPERS
PROTECTIVE GLOVES
DECORATIVE RIBBON (OPTIONAL)
FABRIC SCISSORS (OPTIONAL)

Flower Prep

BERZELIA

Remove all foliage, leaving only
the bubble-like berries. Trim on
a 45-degree angle and hydrate
in room temperature water.

4–6"
ROOM TEMP

GARDEN ROSE

Remove all foliage and thorns
from the rose stems. Trim on
a 45-degree angle and hydrate
in room temperature water.

DEEP
WARM

FRITILLARIA, RANUNCULUS

Keep both types of the fritillary as
long in length as possible, trimming
no more than a centimeter or two
from the bottom of the stems.
Remove all foliage from the
Butterfly Ranunculus, retaining
the lateral blooms off the main
stems. Trim on a 45-degree
angle. Hydrate in cold water.

2–4"
COLD

HELLEBORE

Submerge the *Hellebore* in water
to trim on a 45-degree angle and
hydrate in cold water. Store in a floral
cooler or refrigerator until ready to
use (see Floral cooler on page 15).

4–6"
COLD

Shape

1. Blend the stems of buttonbush and the garden rose stems together to create a round shape.

2. Add all 16 snake's head fritillary stems to the bouquet, dispersing them evenly. Keep your grip loose as you add these delicate stems to prevent breakage.

Color

3. Increase the loosely round shape by layering in a soft rosy color with all 9 hellebore stems. Blend the flowers to share the spotlight with—rather than cover up—the buttonbush, roses, and fritillary.

You know, we talk a lot about hydrating stems, but are you hydrated? Now is a good time to take a break to nourish your body.

Depth

4. Position 4 stems of Butterfly Ranunculus to float around the center of the bouquet. Place the remaining 4 stems so they reach out and away, starting from the upper right corner down to the lower right corner.

5. Add the 3 'Plum Bells' fritillary stems to three different points of the bouquet so they stretch in three distinct directions.

6. Finish by securing the stems with bouquet tape. Trim the ends of the stems until even and place in a vase of cold water until ready to use.

Optional

Add a ribbon of your choice. Use fabric
scissors to trim the ends of the ribbon at a
45-degree angle (see Ribbon on page 28).

DIFFICULTY LEVEL
beginner

SEASON
summer

MOOD
romantic

TYRIAN

*T*his floral fantasy comes to life in three acts. First, 'Munstead Wood' roses tease the plot with dark, mysterious petals. The second act is jovial and energetic with pleated puffs of candy-striped flora. The third act takes the velvety garden roses from the first act and the playful sweet peas from the second act and introduces a dramatic arc of *Cosmos* to perform an unforgettable eleven o'clock number. With all three acts played out, we end our show with a stunning finale of pageantry featuring a breathtaking swirl of cerise and Tyrian purple.

INGREDIENTS

12 STEMS
GARDEN ROSE
'MUNSTEAD WOOD'

10 STEMS
SWEET PEA
'SUZY Z'

17 STEMS
COSMOS
'ROSETTA'

COLOR PALETTE

TYRIAN PURPLE   CERISE   VIOLET RED

CHICKEN WIRE
FLORAL CLIPPERS
PIN FROG, SMALL
PROTECTIVE GLOVES
WATERPROOF FLORAL TAPE
WIRE CUTTERS

Flower Prep

GARDEN ROSE

Remove all foliage and thorns
from the rose stems. Trim on
a 45-degree angle and hydrate
in room temperature water.

 **DEEP
ROOM TEMP**

SWEET PEA, COSMOS

Remove all foliage from the sweet
pea and *Cosmos* stems. Trim on a
45-degree angle and hydrate in cold
water. Store in a cool area, floral
cooler, or refrigerator until ready to
use (see Floral cooler on page 15).

 **3–5"
COLD**

Vase Prep

In a small, preferably turquoise
vase (the one pictured is about
4 inches tall by 3½ inches wide),
place a small pin frog. Cover the
pin frog with a chicken wire pillow.
Secure with a floral tape strap.

Shape

1. Build a loose cloud using 11 garden roses of short to medium
   length. This shape should have plenty of open space and feel
   very free in its form. The arrangement should resemble a
   muffin that has had a bite taken out of its top.

2. Use the pin frog to secure 1 final, tall rose just right of center.
   This stem, already loose in its form, should reach up and out
   of the arrangement, making the shape appear a bit skewed to
   the right.

Color

3. Without increasing the overall height of the arrangement,
   position 5 or 6 short sweet pea stems to fill in the gaps
   between the roses.

4. Place the remaining 4 to 5 sweet pea stems into the vase at
   severe angles. Make sure these stems are long, appearing as
   though the sweet peas are trying to stretch the arrangement
   in several directions.

Depth

5. Place the majority of the *Cosmos* stems (about 13 or 14) on
   the right side of the vase. Pull the violet tone to the other side
   of the arrangement by placing 2 or 3 *Cosmos* stems low on
   the left.

6. Place a final, tall *Cosmos* stem just right of center so it shoots
   up and out beyond the tallest rose.

*It may not be the biggest, but it certainly is
beautifulest. No wait, beauteous? Bootylicious?
What's the word? Let's just go with* beautiful.

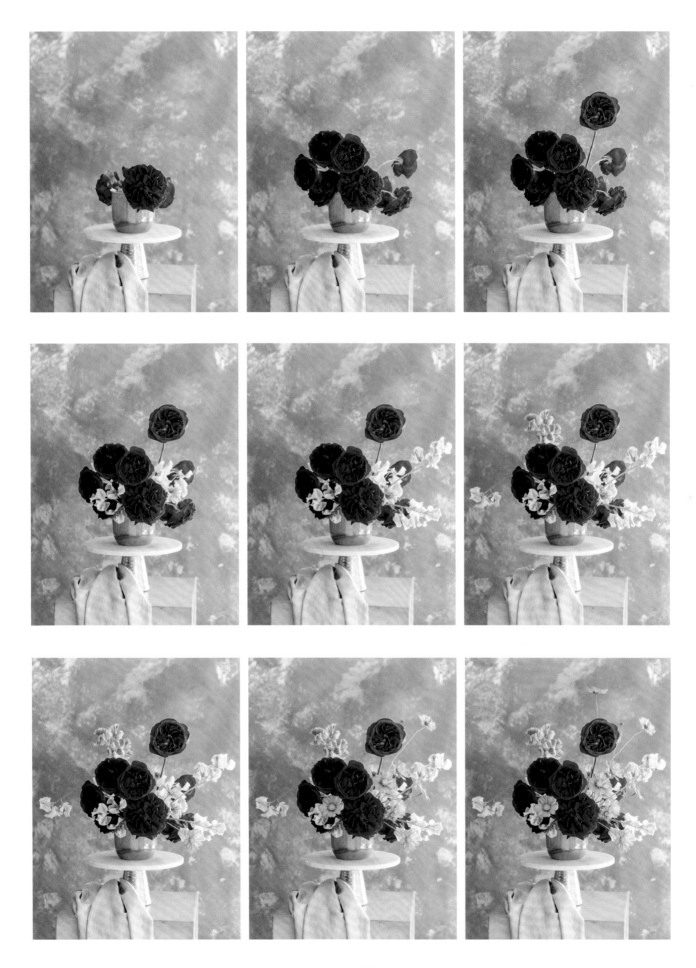

259

Part III

THE FLOWER VAULT

Welcome to the flower vault. Come in. Let yourself get lost in a rainbow of blooms. Here you will find every flower bloom and leaf we have used throughout our journey. All these flowers were sourced from the Seattle Wholesale Growers Market, which gets its products from dozens of local flower farms, mostly on the West Coast. The vault is organized in two sections: first by color and later by season of availability. Check in with your local grower or flower shop to see what's in stock and ask for help if you need recommendations for swaps.

IN CONVERSATION WITH THE SEATTLE WHOLESALE GROWERS MARKET

*A*ll the flowers in this book were sourced locally. I sat down with the team at Seattle Wholesale Growers Market for a little Q&A to learn more about their floral journey and would love to share with you what I learned.

When was the Seattle Wholesale Growers Market established?

In June 2010, a group of Washington and Oregon cut flower farmers met at an industry association gathering to discuss their future. Many were concerned about the viability of their farms. Traditional US floral wholesalers had sharply reduced their local purchases in favor of cheaper, readily available South American imports. Competition was cutting into already thin profit margins and reducing the variety of cut flower material available to floral wholesalers and retailers. The feeling was particularly acute among Seattle-area growers, so a dozen flower farmers from the Pacific Northwest took action to preserve their livelihoods. They pooled their resources and formed the Seattle Wholesale Growers Market Cooperative (SWGMC), a producers' cooperative, to access larger markets. Its mission: to foster a vibrant community marketplace that sustains local flower farms and provides top-quality products and service to the floral industry of the Pacific Northwest. In April 2011, the Seattle Wholesale Growers Market Cooperative opened for business in Seattle's Georgetown neighborhood, also home to the region's major wholesale floral markets for conventional floral goods.

Is there an environmental impact to flower farming?

Absolutely. All our member farms practice sustainable growing practices. Since our producers are local or regional, there is a smaller carbon footprint to produce and deliver the products to market. Foreign flower growers do not have to follow the same environmental standards or labor rules as American farmers. Some blooms never encounter a real bee or butterfly in their short lives, and more than a few are tended by children, despite efforts to eradicate child labor in the industry. Sustainable growing practices benefit the environment and increase biodiversity on the farms.

What are the challenges of growing locally? How do you overcome these challenges?

Seasonal weather patterns and the ever-increasing unknowns with extreme weather conditions play a major role with the production of floral crops. Harvest dates vary from year to year depending on the weather and growing conditions. Fortunately, due to the diversity of microclimates at our farms' locations, we are able to offer floral products over a longer period of time than a usual growing season could provide for a single location.

What is next for Seattle Wholesale Growers Market?

The market is looking beyond the Seattle area, investing more in online capacity, expanding our Northwest delivery areas, and exploring the potential to ship to areas where the local flower industry is relatively undeveloped. One day, we hope to be a member of a new kind of cooperative: a consortium of local grower cooperatives like ourselves, dedicated to supporting and promoting seasonal, sustainable, and stunning local flowers while also encouraging and sustaining the next generation of flower farmers and florists.

Color

GYPSOPHILA (AKA BABY'S BREATH), PINK

JAPANESE *ANEMONE* 'HONORINE JOBERT'

GOMPHRENA GLOBOSA 'QIS PINK'

BUTTERFLY RANUNCULUS 'ARIADNE'

HELLEBORE 'PINK LADY'

ALLIUM SICULUM 'SUMMER BELLS'

GARDEN ROSE 'PIANO FREILAND'

ROSEHIP TIPS 'MAGICAL PEARLS'

ROSE 'ROUGE ROYALE'

RANUNCULUS BUTTERFLY 'HADES'

ANEMONE CORONARIA 'HIS EXCELLENCY'

GARDEN ROSE 'MATADOR'

POINSETTIA 'WINTER ROSE'

DAHLIA 'GARDEN WONDER'

PEONY 'RED CHARM'

GARDEN ROSE 'GRAND JUBILEE'

ASTRANTIA MAJOR
'GILL RICHARDSON'

ROSE
'BLACK BACCARA'

LEUCADENDRON
'EBONY'

SCABIOSA ATROPURPUREA
'BLACKBERRY SCOOP'

AGONIS FLEXUOSA
'JERVIS BAY AFTERDARK'

RANUNCULUS
'CAFÉ AU LAIT'

CELOSIA
'BOMBAY FIRE'

CHRYSANTHEMUM
'BEVERLY BRONZE'

AMARANTH
'HOT BISCUITS'

DAHLIA
'BROWN SUGAR'

CELOSIA
'CELWAY TERRACOTTA'

CHRYSANTHEMUM
'SEATON'S COFFEE'

COTINUS COGGYGRIA (AKA
SMOKETREE) 'YOUNG LADY'

GARDEN ROSE
'KOKO LOKO'

DAHLIA
'POLKA'

DAHLIA
'CAFÉ AU LAIT'

DAHLIA
'A LA MODE'

GARDEN ROSE
'DISTANT DRUM'

MINI CALLA LILY
'PASSION FRUIT'

GARDEN ROSE
'ROMANTIC ANTIKE'

VIOLA
'MARIPOSA'

DAHLIA
'MAGGIE C'

ROSE
'PEACH AVALANCHE'

GARDEN ROSE
'CARAMEL ANTIKE'

PARROT TULIP
'APRICOT'

CELOSIA
'SUPERCREST'

PERSIMMON

ASHBY'S BANKSIA

DATE PALM BERRIES

SPRAY ROSE
'AURELIA'

FREESIA,
'GOLD'

RUDBECKIA
'SAHARA'

PEONY FOLIAGE

FRITILLARIA UVA-VULPIS
(AKA FOX'S GRAPE FRITILLARY)

PINE CONES

KOELREUTERIA PANICULATA
(AKA GOLDEN RAIN TREE) PODS

CURLY WILLOW TIPS

PASSIFLORA INCARNATA
(AKA FRUITING PASSION VINE)

SCABIOSA STELLATA
'STARFLOWER' PODS

SUNFLOWER
'RUBY ECLIPSE'

DRIED TEASEL
'FULLER'S TEASEL'

ANTHRISCUS SYLVESTRIS
'RAVENSWING'

BUTTERFLY DAFFODIL
'ORANGERY'

RANUNCULUS
'TECOLOTE GOLD'

AZTEC
MARIGOLD

RUDBECKIA
'YELLOW CONEFLOWER'

GARDEN ROSE
'YELLOW POMPON'

GARDEN ROSE
'CATALINA'

ALSTROEMERIA
'RIO'

DARWIN DOUBLE TULIP
'AKEBONO'

CHINA ASTER
'TOWER YELLOW'

DAHLIA
'SEATTLE'

MARIGOLD
'WHITE SWAN'

SWEET PEA
'JILLY'

COSMOS
'XANTHOS'

DAHLIA
'YELLOW HEAVEN'

FLOWERING *LYSIMACHIA
CILIATA* 'FIRECRACKER'

PUMPKIN
'TETSUKABUTO'

DAUCUS CAROTA
'CHOCOLATE LACE'

LEYCESTERIA FORMOSA
'GOLDEN LANTERNS'

BANKSIA BAXTERI
(AKA BIRD'S NEST BANKSIA)

CHESTNUT BRANCHES
(WITH SEEDPODS) 'COLOSSAL'

ZINNIA
'QUEEN LIME'

LISIANTHUS
'ROSITA GREEN'

HYDRANGEA
'LIMELIGHT'

BERZELIA LANUGINOSA
(AKA BUTTONBUSH)

NINEBARK FOLIAGE
'DART'S GOLD'

SPIREA
'ARGUTA'

HOPS ON THE VINE
'CASCADE'

'CHOCOLATE MINT'

EUROPEAN PEAR TREE
FOLIAGE

RIBES SANGUINEUM
(AKA RED-FLOWER CURRANT)
FOLIAGE 'KING EDWARD VII'

GERANIUM FOLIAGE
'CHOCOLATE-MINT'

HELLEBORE
'IVORY PRINCE'

CRAB APPLE TIPS

FRESH *QUERCUS RUBRA*
(AKA RED OAK) FOLIAGE

GRAPEVINE TIPS

PRESERVED MOSS

WHEAT
'SILVER TIP'

GLOBE ARTICHOKE
'IMPERIAL STAR'

SEEDED
EUCALYPTUS

PUMPKIN
'BLACK FOREST KABOCHA'

PUMPKIN
'MIDNIGHT'

PEPEROMIA PLANT
'LUNA GREY'

PINUS STROBUS 'CONTORTA'
(AKA CONTORTED WHITE PINE)

CANARY GRASS

LACINATO KALE

TRADESCANTIA
'SILVER PLUS'

PUMPKIN
'JARRAHDALE'

MUSCARI ARMENIACUM
'VALERIE FINNIS'

BLUE RED-OSIER
DOGWOOD BERRIES

DRIED *HYDRANGEA*
'NIGRA'

CYNOGLOSSUM AMABILE
'FIRMAMENT'

NIGELLA
'MISS JEKYLL'

HYACINTH
'DELFT BLUE'

HYACINTH
'BLUE JACKET'

Color

CORNFLOWER
'FOREST BLUE'

DELPHINIUM
'BLUE BIRD'

VIBURNUM TINUS BERRIES
'SPRING BOUQUET'

HELLEBORE
'NEW YORK KNIGHT'

PENNISETUM ALOPECUROIDES
'MOUDRY'

MUSCARI LATIFOLIUM (AKA
GRAPE HYACINTH)

VIOLA 'FRIZZLE SIZZLE
YELLOW-BLUE SWIRL'

ECHINOPS RITRO (AKA GLOBE
THISTLE) 'VEITCH'S BLUE'

ACONITUM CARMICHAELII
'ARENDSII'

ANEMONE
'MR. FOKKER'

CLARY SAGE
'BLUE MONDAY'

HYACINTHOIDES HISPANICA
'EXCELSIOR'

SWEET PEA
'ROYAL NAVY'

SCABIOSA CAUCASICA
'PERFECTA BLUE'

BEARDED IRIS
'HAUNTED HEART'

CHINA ASTER
'MOONSTONE'

SPRAY ROSE
'BLUE POMPON'

FLOWERING *ANTHRISCUS SYLVESTRIS* 'RAVENSWING'

FRENCH PUSSY WILLOW, SILVER

ASTRANTIA MAJOR 'STAR OF ROYALS'

SCABIOSA 'LAVENDER SCOOP'

FLOWERING *PAULOWNIA TOMENTOSA*

GARDEN ROSE 'STEPHEN RULO'

VERONICASTRUM VIRGINICUM 'PINK GLOW'

RHODODENDRON 'PJM ELITE'

DELPHINIUM 'ASTOLAT'

SCABIOSA ATROPURPUREA 'BLACK KNIGHT'

VIOLA 'HALO VIOLET'

TRACHELIUM CAERULEUM 'BLACK KNIGHT'

SWEET PEA 'NIMBUS'

FRITILLARIA PERSICA (AKA PLUM BELLS FRITILLARY)

SWEET PEA 'DARK PASSION'

FRITILLARIA MELEAGRIS (AKA
SNAKE'S HEAD FRITILLARY)

CORNFLOWER
'CLASSIC MAGIC'

DAHLIA
'DOWNHAM ROYAL'

LILAC
'MONGE'

GARDEN ROSE
'MUNSTEAD WOOD'

VERBASCUM × HYBRIDA
'SOUTHERN CHARM'

COSMOS
'ROSETTA'

BUTTERFLY RANUNCULUS
'HERA'

POMPON *DAHLIA*
'BURLESCA'

SWEET PEA
'SUZY Z'

AQUILEGIA VULGARIS (AKA
COLUMBINE) 'PINK PETTICOAT'

MINI POMPON *DAHLIA*
'SMALL WORLD'

PUMPKIN
'CASPERITA'

GOMPHRENA GLOBOSA
'QIS WHITE'

POMPON *DAHLIA*
'WHITE ASTER'

FREESIA,
WHITE

Winter

BUTTERFLY RANUNCULUS
'HADES'

ANEMONE CORONARIA
'HIS EXCELLENCY'

GARDEN
ROSE
'MATADOR'

POINSETTIA
'WINTER ROSE'

ROSE
'BLACK BACCARA'

ASHBY'S BANKSIA

PINE CONES

DRIED TEASEL
'FULLER'S TEASEL'

GARDEN ROSE
'YELLOW POMPON'

DAUCUS CAROTA
'CHOCOLATE LACE'

GERANIUM FOLIAGE
'CHOCOLATE-MINT'

SEEDED *EUCALYPTUS*

PEPEROMIA PLANT
'LUNA GREY'

PINUS STROBUS 'CONTORTA'
(AKA CONTORTED WHITE PINE)

MUSCARI ARMENIACUM
'VALERIE FINNIS'

DRIED *HYDRANGEA*
'NIGRA'

CORNFLOWER
'FOREST BLUE'

HELLEBORE
'NEW YORK KNIGHT'

ANEMONE
'MR. FOKKER'

SCABIOSA CAUCASICA
'PERFECTA BLUE'

FRENCH PUSSY WILLOW,
SILVER

Spring

BUTTERFLY RANUNCULUS
'ARIADNE'

HELLEBORE
'PINK LADY'

ALLIUM BULGARICUM
'SUMMER BELLS'

PEONY
'RED CHARM'

GARDEN ROSE
'GRAND JUBILEE'

ASTRANTIA MAJOR
'GILL RICHARDSON'

RANUNCULUS
'CAFÉ AU LAIT'

GARDEN ROSE
'KOKO LOKO'

GARDEN ROSE
'DISTANT DRUM'

GARDEN ROSE
'ROMANTIC ANTIKE'

VIOLA
'MARIPOSA'

PARROT TULIP
'APRICOT'

SPRAY ROSE
'AURELIA'

FREESIA, GOLD

FRITILLARIA UVA-VULPIS
(AKA FOX'S GRAPE FRITILLARY)

ANTHRISCUS SYLVESTRIS
'RAVENSWING'

BUTTERFLY DAFFODIL
'ORANGERY'

RANUNCULUS
'TECOLOTE GOLD'

GARDEN ROSE
'CATALINA'

ALSTROEMERIA
'RIO'

DARWIN DOUBLE TULIP
'AKEBONO'

BERZELIA LANUGINOSA
(AKA BUTTONBUSH), GREEN

NINEBARK FOLIAGE
'DART'S GOLD'

SPIREA
'ARGUTA'

HELLEBORE
'IVORY PRINCE'

TRADESCANTIA ZEBRINA
'SILVER PLUS'

HYACINTH
'DELFT BLUE'

HYACINTH
'BLUE JACKET'

MUSCARI LATIFOLIUM (AKA
GRAPE HYACINTH), DARK BLUE

VIOLA 'FRIZZLE SIZZLE
YELLOW-BLUE SWIRL'

CYNOGLOSSUM AMABILE
'FIRMAMENT'

HYACINTHOIDES HISPANICA
'EXCELSIOR'

SWEET PEA
'ROYAL NAVY'

BEARDED IRIS
'HAUNTED HEART'

FLOWERING ANTHRISCUS
SYLVESTRIS 'RAVENSWING'

ASTRANTIA MAJOR
'STAR OF ROYALS'

SCABIOSA
'LAVENDER SCOOP'

FLOWERING
PAULOWNIA TOMENTOSA

RHODODENDRON
'PJM ELITE'

DELPHINIUM
'ASTOLAT'

SCABIOSA ATROPURPUREA
'BLACK KNIGHT'

VIOLA
'HALO VIOLET'

FRITILLARIA PERSICA (AKA
FRITILLARY) 'PLUM BELLS'

SWEET PEA
'DARK PASSION'

FRITILLARIA MELEAGRIS (AKA
SNAKE'S HEAD FRITILLARY)

LILAC
'MONGE'

VERBASCUM × HYBRIDA
'SOUTHERN CHARM'

BUTTERFLY RANUNCULUS
'HERA'

AQUILEGIA VULGARIS (AKA
COLUMBINE) 'PINK PETTICOAT'

FREESIA, WHITE

Summer

GYPSOPHILA
(AKA BABY'S BREATH), PINK

JAPANESE *ANEMONE*
'HONORINE JOBERT'

GOMPHRENA GLOBOSA
'QIS PINK'

GARDEN ROSE
'PIANO FREILAND'

DAHLIA
'GARDEN WONDER'

CELOSIA
'BOMBAY FIRE'

AMARANTH
'HOT BISCUITS'

DAHLIA
'BROWN SUGAR'

CELOSIA
'CELWAY TERRACOTTA'

COTINUS COGGYGRIA (AKA
SMOKETREE) 'YOUNG LADY'

DAHLIA
'POLKA'

DAHLIA
'CAFÉ AU LAIT'

DAHLIA
'A LA MODE'

MINI CALLA LILLY
'PASSION FRUIT'

DAHLIA
'MAGGIE C'

GARDEN ROSE
'CARAMEL ANTIKE'

CELOSIA
'SUPERCREST'

PEONY FOLIAGE

PASSIFLORA INCARNATA
(AKA FRUITING PASSION VINE)

SCABIOSA STELLATA
(AKA STARFLOWER) PODS

AZTEC MARIGOLD

RUDBECKIA 'YELLOW
CONEFLOWER'

CHINA ASTER
'TOWER YELLOW'

DAHLIA
'SEATTLE'

MARIGOLD
'WHITE SWAN'

SWEET PEA
'JILLY'

COSMOS
'XANTHOS'

DAHLIA
'YELLOW HEAVEN'

FLOWERING *LYSIMACHIA CILIATA*
'FIRECRACKER'

LEYCESTERIA FORMOSA
'GOLDEN LANTERNS'

CHESTNUT BRANCHES
(WITH SEEDPODS) 'COLOSSAL'

ZINNIA
'QUEEN LIME'

LISIANTHUS
'ROSITA GREEN'

HYDRANGEA
'LIMELIGHT'

HOPS ON THE VINE
'CASCADE'

'CHOCOLATE MINT'

EUROPEAN PEAR TREE FOLIAGE

RIBES SANGUINEUM
'KING EDWARD VII'

CRAB APPLE TIPS

FRESH *QUERCUS RUBRA*
(AKA RED OAK) FOLIAGE

GRAPEVINE TIPS

GLOBE ARTICHOKE
'IMPERIAL STAR'

NIGELLA
'MISS JEKYLL'

ECHINOPS RITRO (AKA GLOBE
THISTLE) 'VEITCH'S BLUE'

CLARY SAGE
'BLUE MONDAY'

CHINA ASTER
'MOONSTONE'

SPRAY ROSE
'BLUE POMPON'

GARDEN ROSE
'STEPHEN RULO'

VERONICASTRUM VIRGINICUM
'PINK GLOW'

TRACHELIUM CAERULEUM
'BLACK KNIGHT'

SWEET PEA
'NIMBUS'

CORNFLOWER
'CLASSIC MAGIC'

DAHLIA
'DOWNHAM ROYAL'

GARDEN ROSE
'MUNSTEAD WOOD'

COSMOS
'ROSETTA'

POMPON DAHLIA
'BURLESCA'

SWEET PEA
'SUZY Z'

POMPON *DAHLIA*
'WHITE ASTER'

Autumn

ROSEHIP TIPS
'MAGICAL PEARLS'

ROSE
'ROUGE ROYALE'

LEUCADENDRON
'EBONY'

SCABIOSA ATROPURPUREA
'BLACKBERRY SCOOP'

AGONIS FLEXUOSA
'JERVIS BAY AFTERDARK'

CHRYSANTHEMUM
'BEVERLY BRONZE'

CHRYSANTHEMUM
'SEATON'S COFFEE'

ROSE
'PEACH AVALANCHE'

PERSIMMON

DATE PALM BERRIES

RUDBECKIA
'SAHARA'

KOELREUTERIA PANICULATA
(AKA GOLDEN RAIN TREE) PODS

CURLY WILLOW TIPS

SUNFLOWER
'RUBY ECLIPSE'

PUMPKIN
'TETSUKABUTO'

BANKSIA BAXTERI
(AKA BIRD'S NEST BANKSIA)

PRESERVED MOSS

WHEAT
'SILVER TIP'

WINTER SQUASH
'BLACK FOREST KABOCHA'

PUMPKIN 'MIDNIGHT'

CANARY GRASS

LACINATO KALE

PUMPKIN
'JARRAHDALE'

BLUE RED-OSIER
DOGWOOD BERRIES

VIBURNUM TINUS BERRIES
'SPRING BOUQUET'

DELPHINIUM
'BLUE BIRD'

PENNISETUM ALOPECUROIDES
'MOUDRY'

ACONITUM CARMICHAELII
'ARENDSII'

MINI POMPON DAHLIA
'SMALL WORLD'

PUMPKIN
'CASPERITA'

GOMPHRENA GLOBOSA
'QIS WHITE'

ACKNOWLEDGMENTS

While I would love to take all the credit and pretend that this book magicked itself into reality, there is no way this floral fantasy could have been possible if it were not for the help of many, many, many people. To my editors and to other key figures in my life and career I say, THANK YOU!

To Liz DeCesare: You are a rare breed of human whose generosity, council, and friendship continually uplifts everyone around you. Myself included. I know that I am unworthy of your expertise but that won't stop me from hoarding it like a chipmunk hoards nuts. I could not have dreamed for a better manager and partner. THANK YOU!

To Sara Neville: I said this the first time we met and I still believe it to this day, "We would have been best friends in high school." You just get it. You immediately understood what this book was about and you gave me the confidence to finish. Your brilliance as an editor has elevated this project beyond what I thought was possible. Thank you for the never-ending nudge towards reaching my full potential. If you think that our friendship ends with the closing of this book, you've got another thing coming. I adore and respect you, so much!! THANK YOU!

To the team at Clarkson Potter: Mia Johnson, Jenny Beal Davis, Heather Williamson, Joyce Wong, Brianne Sperber, and Jana Branson. I could not have asked for a better pit crew. Without you my wheels would have fallen off a long time ago. THANK YOU!

To the staff at Seattle Wholesale Growers Market: Brad, Katy, Cerisse, Wan Chi, and all the amazing farmers—you are just the best. Your dedication to growing and harvesting the most beautiful creations the earth has to offer astounds me. There is no possible way to express how integral the SWGM has been in the creation of this text. This whole book is really a love letter to the floral community here in Washington. Sure, the designs are cute, but it is your product that is the real star! THANK YOU!

To Haley Heidemann: How did I get so lucky to have you as my agent? Having you in my corner gave me the confidence to become the artist I imagined myself to be when I was a child. It's like walking into a restaurant with my hot sauce in my bag: no matter the circumstances, you make everything better. THANK YOU!

To Aaron Griffith-VanderYacht: Whenever I thought that I couldn't, you told me I could. Whenever I called an arrangement trash, you showed me it was gold. Whenever I needed a hand, you gave me yours (no literally, your hand is in like half of these pictures holding flowers!!). You are incredible, and if it were not for your support, I would probably still be circling the drain waiting for someone to push me into my dream life. With you I am there! THANK YOU!

To my boys: The thought of leaving behind a legacy for you to carry forward was all the motivation I needed to push through the sleepless nights, calloused hands, dried-out tears, and wilted blooms. All of this is for you. Your love is the sunshine of my life. I have bloomed into the person I am today because of you. I am so proud and lucky to be your dad and to call you mine. I love you. THANK YOU!

Published in the United States by Clarkson Potter/
Publishers, an imprint of Random House, a division of
Penguin Random House LLC, New York.
ClarksonPotter.com
RandomHouseBooks.com

CLARKSON POTTER is a trademark and POTTER with
colophon is a registered trademark of Penguin Random
House LLC.

Library of Congress Control Number: 2022944726

ISBN 978-0-593-23496-9
Ebook ISBN 978-0-593-23497-6

Printed in China

Photographer: Kristen Griffith-VanderYacht
Editor: Sara Neville
Designer: Mia Johnson
Production Editor: Joyce Wong
Production Manager: Heather Williamson
Compositor: Merri Ann Morrell
Copy Editor: Natalie Blachere
Marketer: Brianne Sperber
Publicist: Jana Branson

Cover design by Mia Johnson and Jennifer K. Beal Davis
Cover photographs by Kristen Griffith-VanderYacht

10 9 8 7 6 5 4 3 2 1

First Edition